MEMOIR OF A FRIEND

BOOKS BY HERBERT MASON

A Legend of Alexander and *The Merchant and the Parrot*,
 Dramatic Poems

The Death of al-Hallaj, a Dramatic Narrative

Gilgamesh, a Verse Narrative

Summer Light, a Novel

Moments in Passage, a Memoir

The Passion of al-Hallaj by Louis Massignon, 4 vols.
 (translator)

Two Statesmen of Mediaeval Islam, a Study

Reflections on the Middle East Crisis (editor)

Memoir of a Friend:

LOUIS MASSIGNON

by Herbert Mason

UNIVERSITY OF NOTRE DAME PRESS
NOTRE DAME, INDIANA

Quotations from letters of Thomas Merton to the author
are used with the permission of the Merton Legacy Trust.

Library of Congress Cataloging-in-Publication Data

Mason, Herbert, 1932-
    Memoir of a friend, Louis Massignon.

    Includes bibliographical references.
    1. Massignon, Louis, 1883-1962.
2. Orientalists—France—Biography. 3. Mason,
Herbert,   1932-   —Diaries. 4. Scholars,
Muslim—France—Biography. 5. Orientalists—
United States—Diaries. I. Title.
BP49.5.M3M37 1987   297'.092'4   [B]   87-40349
ISBN 0-268-01365-9

Manufactured in the United States of America

In memory of LOUIS MASSIGNON
1883-1962

In appreciation of JOHN D. BARRETT, JR.
1905-1981,
whose devotion to Louis Massignon and
determination to publish his *La Passion d'al-Hallaj*
made possible the transmission of his thought
and work in America.

CONTENTS

FOREWORD

The two years of 1959 and 1960, when I knew Louis Massignon on an almost daily basis, were my most attentive, impressionable, and receptive years. A year before, in 1958, at the age of twenty-six, I had converted formally to Roman Catholicism from the Episcopalianism of my family heritage; never before or since have I been so open to new people and new ideas. Our meeting and ensuing friendship, which continued through letters until his death, October 31, 1962, and to the present day through my work of translation of his magnum opus, *La Passion d'al-Hallaj*, and my own writing on themes of mutual interest, nevertheless served no useful purpose in an ordinary mundane sense. Our association led to no job and promised no rewards. In a truly Taoist sense it was outside the realm of usefulness.

Louis Massignon, however, was not esoteric or ethereal and bore no aura of the mystical or magical guru about him. To those who knew him at his height he was an august, disciplined, and intense scholar of the Collège de France. Even though he had retired by the time I met him, I had been apprised of his distinguished position

---

*Published as *The Passion of al-Hallaj* in the Bollingen Series, Princeton University Press, 4 vols., 1982.

in French learning and warned by a few friends of his power to influence and possess. But I had no intention of studying any of the fields of his expertise and no qualifications for doing so had the intent been there. I was protected, I believed, by a mixture of ignorance and lack of fear at my vulnerability.

Recently, after reviewing for the first time the diary I kept of the years 1958 through 1968, when I began to edit and translate his great work on al-Hallaj, I realized the kind of learning I gained from those two years of our meetings and friendship. What emerged primarily is an informal portrait of the teacher himself.

Since the present book is in one sense a dialogue between Louis Massignon and myself, it may be appropriate to digress for a moment to introduce myself. I was born in 1932 in Wilmington, Delaware, of parents of some artistic and religious temperament but whose occupations — both my father's and, following his death, my mother's — were that of paper manufacturer, mill owner, in a word, business. I was the younger of two children. My sister is an artist and book illustrator. The scenery of our childhood was principally that of Maryland's Eastern Shore. Our property included an old riverboat docking point jutting out into the convergence of the Choptank and Tuckahoe Rivers. The scenery was alive with many species of animals, birds, flowers, trees, sunsets, and always the rivers. Because of my early experience and parental tutelage I was at home in the world of nature, not of ideas or of sophisticated conceptualized learning. Still, I did go to fairly conventional schools, attended my father's and his brothers' college, Harvard, where I majored in English. I read widely in literature, history, philosophy, and art of different cultures, and I discovered that I liked to write and that I intended to write narrative poetry, that is, not long fragmentary autobiographical poems or sequences of short poems, but stories with plots told in rhythmic verse rather than prose. I lived more intimately at college with Homer's *Iliad* and *Odyssey* than with my roommates. The power and economy of the metrics and the structuring of the story lines absorbed and spoiled my taste for prose forms that took needless time and words to unfold and be resolved. The classical epic's intense sense of timing and of condensed time was right to my ear. My greatest excitement was the discovery of the story of Gilgamesh. Though it survives only in fragments of ancient adaptations and retellings of still more ancient lost sources, it seemed to me instantly whole and corresponded to my sense of kindredness with nature, my experience of loss caused by my father's death, and my appreciation of the friendships that, with time, restored my affection for life.

Gilgamesh captivated me and I came away wanting more than anything to retell the story. This wish took form in me as a narrative quest. And with nothing more than this to guide me, I went abroad, as if under the guiding form and spell of the narrative itself, to meet a strange and distant wise man who, as the fragments indicate, "had seen all things," the Utnapishtim of the story, who might give me the secret of eternal life, or failing that, of accepting my life as it had come to be.

I have postponed the present book for many years, perhaps because it is so personal, perhaps because I needed time to complete the cycle of Massignon's prodigious research into the life, martyrdom, and teaching of the tenth-century poet and mystic, al-Hallaj. My work on the translation of Massignon's study not only allowed

3

me to know Massignon as the teacher of my quest but also brought me to al-Hallaj, who had been the teacher of his.

In those two years of 1959 and 1960 most of the writing that I did was in the form of a diary. The energy and person of Louis Massignon consumed my creativity and postponed the work I had gone there to do. Friendship can risk the postponement and even the loss of one's plans, but it can also open up new worlds which exceed our undertaking and possession. Such was the effect of Massignon's influence and friendship on me and it is with a sense of his continuing presence that I write now of that friend and that time.

PART ONE

Massignon, an Introduction with Commentary on His Major Themes and Thought

1

There are many accounts of the life of Louis Massignon, and studies of his thought continue to be written. Portions of his wide and varied correspondence have been published. Expressions of admiration for, and criticism of, his scholarship abound. He was honored richly during his lifetime and the centenary of his birth has been commemorated by his country. Medal engravings of his face have been struck; schools and streets have been named for him at home and abroad; his disciples and his detractors carry on their respective supererogations of devotion and dismantling. He is officially dead. I do not wish to add to this post mortem process.

If the process could be reversed and he could be brought magically back to life, I would want him to be as scrappy, unpredictable, indefinable, elusive, and outrageous as he was in life, at least as he was when I knew him. But my fear about such reversals is that he would return as a subject for study, as "a body, not a life," to quote Shakespeare. In life it was his passion for love itself that made his "immortal longings" ring true and defy others' comprehension. He was not a saint, prophet, or a hero, but he was not simply an ordinary person either. Some have called him a "genius," based on his early mastery of foreign and especially oriental languages, his amazing knack for discovering texts in remote places where others never bothered or dared to go and that others declared never existed or were no longer extant, and his rare gifts of deciphering, interpreting, and translating these elusive texts.

He was declared "original" while barely twenty and had received all imaginable academic and professional accolades by thirty. By then he had already made significant discoveries during numerous "missions" abroad, in Islamic lands especially. He had undergone a religious conversion (some say, mistakenly, from disbelief to Islam, then later from Islam to his maternal tradition, Roman Catholicism), published the kernals of his major researches and ideas, established his important lifelong friendships, become a professor of Arabic in Egypt, and was about to be married to his cousin, Marcelle Dansaert-Testelin, by whom there would be two sons and a daughter (Yves, 1915–1935; Daniel, 1919; and Geneviève, 1921–1966), each destined for distinction in his or her own field of scientific research. After the war, in which he served first in the *service de presse* and afterwards by his own request as a frontlines officer (in the Dardanelles, Macedonia, and Serbia), he worked for George Picot, the French High Commissioner for the Occupied Territories of Palestine and Syria. It was then too that he met the already fabled T. E. Lawrence.* It appears to have been a meeting of contrasts: Massignon, at age thirty-four, the established Arabic scholar of exceptional gifts, Lawrence, at age twenty-nine, the ambiguous but celebrated adventurer. The former referred to the latter in an article as "almost an outlaw." Lawrence makes no mention of the meeting in his writings.

---

*See Albert Hourani, "T.E. Lawrence and Louis Massignon," *TLS*, July 8, 1983, 733–734; and *Presence de Louis Massignon* (Paris, 1987), pp. 167–176.

After a brief period, in 1919, of serving the French government under Clemenceau as representative of the Middle East, he became "professeur": first, from 1919 to 1924, "Professeur suppléant" to the chair in Islamic Sociology at the Collège de France, and thereafter, in 1926, the chair holder himself. The assortment of honors, directorships, editorships, memberships, to say nothing of his list of pioneering scholarly books, articles, translations, editions, reviews, and his worldwide correspondence from 1926 until his retirement in 1954, justified his early acclaim and indeed exceeded it. This is the period of his widest recognition, the basis of his becoming officially established in the professionally and generally learned worlds. The American philanthropist Paul Mellon (who along with his first wife, Mary, "discovered" Massignon through their participation during the 1930s in the Eranos Conferences at Ascona, Switzerland) has remarked "I have always thought of him as the ideal of the scholar-philosopher." At Ascona he was considered a "spell-binder." The late John D. Barrett, a close friend of the Mellons and their choice for director of the Bollingen Series, was wholly devoted to him, recounting often the evenings when Massignon held his audiences "entranced with the range of his learning and the depth of his religious understanding." Those who "knew him *then*," as I did not, except as I came to later and indirectly through his works, say that was "the real Massignon," the Massignon whose mind and presence were awesome, indeed peerless. Certainly no one in France or perhaps even in Europe or abroad equaled his mastery in Arabic research and, among non-Muslims in particular, his penetration and affirmation of the sources of Islam. He contributed greatly to the Western recognition of the Qur'an's authenticity as a religious text, however presumptive that claim should sound to us now. Considering the general European contrary view reflected by popes, crusaders, common folk, Dante, Voltaire, and many others, his was a daring position to take and to stand by to the end of his life. Still, this was the Massignon of "genius," not the Massignon of the late period that I knew who was often dismissed and reviled for his "political engagements." I must add that Jack Barrett, to his great credit, tolerated this latter phase of Massignon's life as several others did not, partly because of his own admiration for the man's consistently unpredictable "curve of life."

What was the nature and range of his thought that became so immediately and widely noted? This question has begun to elicit responses from students of the history of ideas, sociology, religion, psychology, comparative oriental and occidental studies, comparative Semitic studies, Islamic and Arabic studies, and it is certain to elicit more. I shall suggest only a few lines of inquiry and draw very few conclusions here. I have both the advantage and disadvantage of having known him, though not in his most celebrated years, and it is therefore difficult for me to analyze him. Nevertheless, I shall consider first what was evident throughout his life: his native gifts, the tools at his command.

He had extraordinary linguistic abilities: he read several dozen languages, spoke perhaps ten of these fluently, and knew the classical roots and contemporary idioms of each. He could communicate in the style of aristocrats or laborers, and was in effect a linguistic chameleon, though not out of desire to hide in the costumes of foreigners but because of his genuine interest in languages for their own sake and in language itself as the source of a people's formulations of ideas and understanding of experience. His primary concentration was on the

Semitic family of languages, especially Arabic, which he believed had preserved the most archaic elements of the Semitic syntactical structure and therefore, though historically the youngest of the major Semitic languages, was the one preserving the earliest formulations of Semitic thought. In Arabic especially, he studied the Semitic origins of root forms, conceptions of time in rhythmic and metrical patterns, and balance of the Semitic fixed grammatical principles with the flexibility needed to assimilate new and foreign linguistic materials.

If Massignon had confined himself to the realm of Semitic language study alone, his place in scholarship would have been secure; and some believe, in any case, it is the realm of his major contribution. However, it was from this primary source and textual medium of study that he became intrigued by the evolution of ritual from language and the assimilation of religious phenomena by linguistic structures. Some linguistic structures re-formed phenomena into general philosophical concepts, others into intimate and popular proverbs. For him both were expressions of historical development and social understanding. His own taste ran to the proverbial, folkloric, and mythic formulations found in the earliest cultures of the Near East.

His personal sense of "correspondences" led him to remarkable instances of archetypal recurrences found in ancient non-Semitic cultures, such as Iranian, Greek, and Celtic. Though such comparative studies were not his main concern, they revealed his dazzling ability to ground himself in sources and yet retain a flexibility of inquiry into almost anything. He himself was immediately alive to new information, yet was inwardly cautious. He had simultaneously the imagination of a poet and the authority of a scientist. Such a combination seems impossible, perhaps even an irreconcilable contradiction. His ignoring of the contradiction, his defiant presence in exciting fusion, was what I believe gave him his special aura among poets and scholars and their amateur appreciators and patrons. Among common people who met him as an inquiring guest and listened as he spoke appreciatively of their distinct and rich traditions and ways, whether in Turkey, Iraq, Morocco, Uganda, Russia, Japan, or Brittany, his personal blend of scientist and poet was not as apparent as his ease in honoring their hospitality. When he addressed small circles of intellectuals in Paris or in other centers of European, Soviet, or American civilization, he communicated his sources evocatively and respectfully as if still *in situ* and thus conveyed the experience of being there to others. His rhetorical power grounded in firsthand learning, his wit and playfulness with the rich and established, made him an instant "spellbinder."

He had exceptional gifts in the French language, which he expressed most poetically in his interpretive prose-poem translations of Arabic mystical poetry and accounts of the mystics' lives. Students have begun to diagnose Massignon's contribution to modern French literature and anthologists have included him among their lyric selections. He used the word *literary*, however, in a pejorative sense and considered literary people, in general, derivative and of only secondary interest. He wrote poems as a young man, but as he told me once, he "destroyed them all" in his twenties. The few poems he did write later were eloquent "imitations" in the Persian mystical vein. His early act of renouncing any "absorption" with his own poetry or fiction bore the stamp of a moral and vocational obligation and was indeed a real sacrifice that caused him pain. For poets, however, he retained a certain admira-

12

tion and quoted generously from the works of those contemporaries he knew personally and of those "classics" he revered.

He was clearly learned in Western as well as in Islamic and other Eastern literatures, again a chameleon absorbed by and absorbing of the color tones and rhythms of each. He appreciated writers for their linguistic gifts, not for effete inclinations or forays into political or religious prophethood. Renunciation was aimed at his own erroneousness, not at his or others' particular and diverse origins. He also believed one's critics and enemies were often more insightful in their ongoing and concentrated evaluations than were one's supporters and friends. Hence, one of his modes of historical re-creation was to rely heavily on the testimonies of the enemies of those persons whose writings or lives attracted him. He startled with such accounts that seemed to put his own subjects and theses about them in jeopardy. I think he had a predisposition, at a level much deeper than Lawrence's, for the dangerous and forbidden and was not afraid of the risks and self-sacrifices required to cross frontiers.

In addition to his linguistic gifts and knowledge of languages, he had a remarkable memory: a seemingly limitless storehouse of major and minor information, and a breathless power of multi-digressive recall. For one thing, Massignon never seemed physically or intellectually tired. He also never appeared bored. Others were always primary sources of knowledge to him—at least about themselves. Students were bearers of exciting new perspectives—that educated *him*. With this consuming and sometimes naive enthusiasm he could be overwhelming to some people. Just as one sensed a pause coming and a relief from intensity, he drew on a hidden reserve and began an entire new exploration. He could leave listeners limp.

My first view of Massignon was in just such a state, for the audience—which on that occasion was large, crowded into Salle Richelieu of the Sorbonne on the evening of March 18, 1959 for a kind of celebration of the friendship of Charles de Foucauld and Louis Massignon and, to be sure, a call for an end to the war in Algeria. The speakers included a number of French and Algerian notables, only two of whom—the philosopher Gabriel Marcel and the novelist Julien Green—were familiar names to me. The occasion was billed as a commemoration of the life and thought of the French ascetic Charles de Foucauld, who was assassinated in the Moroccan desert near Tamanrasset on December 1, 1916. Foucauld had left a "rule of life," which his friend Louis Massignon edited in 1928, for a possible new religious order of brothers and sisters who would work and live side by side with the poorest and most overlooked of society's people. Foucauld's writings were excerpted for the occasion but were read in an unfortunately stilted manner by an actor of the Comédie Française, who could not give feelings to the words. Nor could most who followed in their varied callings for an end to the "fratricidal war"— the French Ministre de Justice Michelet, a black-robed Muslim shaykh from Algeria, a white-robed Christian White Father from Morocco, Marcel, and Green—until the last speaker, a retired *professeur* of the Collège de France dressed in a black three-piece academic suit, Louis Massignon, who clearly felt the words. This last speaker addressed the already exhausted audience for over an hour. A Franciscan friar seated to my left, who had slept through the preliminaries, sat wide awake, his eyes riveted to the speaker's platform. We were collectively

14

carried through states of laughter and sorrow by the speaker's animated facial expressions, hand gestures, words of recollection, and above all vivid evocations of Foucauld himself, whom he alone of the speakers had personally known and visited in the desert. Indeed, he alone *knew* Algeria, North Africa, the Muslim world. His was the presence of a learned man, but more important, also a compassionate man.

The evening showed a man of vivid memories but also of powerful understandings, whose passion for justice lacked any hint of cliché. On this and later occasions at which I was present and in his written works involving the subject of justice, he was consistent: first, in his adherence to sources: to a people's particular modes of thinking and characteristic cultural formulations; second, in his avoidance of imposing general principles from without. He was perhaps the only man at that time who could speak with equal knowledge of both French and Algerian values and guide his listeners' concentration respectfully to each. Perhaps others could, but he actually did.

On the one hand, the position he took was instinctive: he recognized suffering and wanted most to end it wherever and to whomever it occurred. On the other hand, both his courage and his understanding evolved over many years through painstaking work and devotion to sources beyond himself. The man on the platform was not an enshrined genius but a man like other men, a witness denuded, frustrated, and saddened by the times. He was exceptional in that he spoke the languages, he knew the sources, of both people's mythical and historical consciousness and of their specific formulations of ideals. He shared their frustrations in being thwarted, internally and externally, in the realization of those ideals. When he spoke of justice, he spoke first and in rare detail of

15

the people and society who were seeking it. He distrusted talks "on justice" as a subject transcending and indifferent to historical context, for these served only to keep justice itself from becoming palpably accessible. Such talks nurtured doubt about the practicality of justice. Such doubt was the disposition and practice of the French majority of his time.

His initial position on France *vis-à-vis* Algeria, dating from the period after World War II when he was also an emissary of the provisional government of the French Republic to the Near East, was that of host to guest, calling for "respect as a human right" and for the redressing of Algerian Muslim grievances. He also recognized France's long presence in Algeria and the humanly understandable claims of the *pied-noirs*. Only much later, and then only after the outbreak of the war in 1954, did he recognize sadly the inevitability of Algerian independence.* That same year he retired from the Collège de France and gave up all forms of officialdom once and for all. He lectured for the last time at Ascona in 1955, when he violated his director's, Olga Froebe's, ban on

---

*In the period of 1945-46 with Kabylie revolts, which left 10,000 Algerians dead, Massignon went to the government to protest the French reaction. Subsequent revolts and reactions were all met with statements against French violence by Massignon published in *Le Monde*. His action was always for "respect as a human right" rather than a call for Algerian independence. He was not a political insurgent. He was arguing in that period for Algerian Muslims' rights as Frenchmen. After Mendès-France granted independence to Tunisia in 1954, extremist groups of French settlers gained increasing power in Algeria. In France, Robert Schuman, as Ministre de Justice, rejected negotiations to resolve matters of injustice and called for European support of a French Algeria, which spirit Massignon decried. (Pierre Gabriel of Part Two was closely associated with Robert Schuman.)

16

politics by discussing the Algerian Crisis, one among many world crises which the Eranos conferences were not designed to discuss.* Thus began the period of "the later Massignon."

From 1954 until the Algerian war's conclusion in 1962, he was immersed in unofficial teaching and in actions designed to make both sides recognize the humanity of each other and in witnessing justice and compassion for both. His efforts consumed and finally exhausted him. Indeed, he died shortly after the war's conclusion.

His earlier period of "Massignon the genius" or "the real Massignon" is not "another Massignon," but rather his later period marks the assent to action by a man whose ideas held the seeds of that action long before at a level of risk not realized by his early admirers. Among his unofficial actions for fraternal peace was the founding of the prayer sodality of "substitutes," the *Badaliya*, in Damietta, Egypt, as early as 1934. It was with this group in the fall of 1961 that he made "the cry of Antigone,"** following an incident in which French police in Paris had shot some Algerian "suspects" and thrown their bodies in the Seine. He and his fellow *Badaliya* members attempted to recover the bodies from the river in order to give them a proper Muslim rite of burial. He also had become drawn to the teachings of Gandhi prior to World War II, visited the site of his "last pilgrimage" at Mehrauli, India, in 1953, and presided over the *Amis de Gandhi* Society from 1954 until his death. Although he was a

---

*See W. McGuire, *Bollingen, An Adventure in Collecting the Past* (Princeton, 1982), p. 154.

**Le Monde*, October 18, 1961. The event occurred the previous day.

weekly visitor to North Africans detained in prisons from 1955 until 1962, he had already been visiting prisons for many years before the Algerian War to teach basic French and economics to immigrant Muslim workers. And of course there was the teaching of al-Hallaj, whose works he had come to know as early as 1907. Clearly he was not the Massignon of old — except to those who knew him well from the beginning. His life was an unfolding itinerary or, in his own word, a "curve" (*une courbe*), not a fixed or static position he himself had achieved. Like the Arabic verb, his root was a specific invariable structure whose potential for elaboration awaited only certain syntactical additions and for animation only the subtle inbreathing of certain spiritually informed vowels. When called to by the sufferings of others, the word he enacted was *compassion*. The turning of an indifferent ear by one not deaf was to him an act of falsehood. Cultivation of falsehood in defense of national security was an act of dishonor. Draining the resources of another's community to enhance one's own was an act of injustice. And the use of any language to deceive was a betrayal of the essence of human intercourse. Language itself reveals what is in the heart.

The gift of language was for Massignon his primary subject, theme, and tool of inquiry. More than any other force in his life, it led him to the study of Islam and its traditions, to experientially explore the Qur'an, to study, collect, and comment on the lexicon of technical words used by adepts of Islam's mystical tradition, especially in its earliest development, and most notably to investigate the biographical and legal sources involved in the life, teaching, trial, and martyrdom of Husayn ibn Mansur, known as *al-Hallaj* or "the reader of hearts." The gift of language for Massignon was also the gift of spiritual insight. The two were virtually synonymous for him, though each possessed distinct qualities, and language of itself did not mean wisdom or prophetic power. He believed that only some — the Semitic — languages had received the latter historically. Others at their best had only the wisdom of poetry. In defending this view he could be very dogmatic as well as insightful. And given the nineteenth-century legacy, especially in scholarship, whether Christian or agnostic, of anti-Semitism as regards language as well as tradition and people, his dogmatism was as necessary as it was to some bizarre. He encountered hostility to his chosen research within his own family — his father supported Egyptology, not Arabic studies, for a career; and he discovered it among scholars, though fortunately not among his major teachers, notably Hartwig Derenbourg and Ignace Goldziher, his chief school friend the great Sinologist Henri Maspero, and his French Catholic compatriot Jacques Maritain. It was his dogmatic linguistic Semitism that led him to declare the authenticity of the Arabic Qur'an as an inspired religious source and this permitted him to believe in and explore the civilization of Islam and its varied peoples as having genuine importance to the history of humankind, indeed to the salvation of the world. Since most Western scholars of Islam approached their subjects without any thought of personal belief exceeding their scientific research, he was left virtually free and alone to explore at risk and at any level he wished or, as many Muslim admirers of his believe, at a level deeper than any Westerner before him had gone. It is as a reverent witness thus, not merely as a scholar per se, that he is most admired still in the Islamic world; indeed, he became for many Muslims in North Africa and the Near East, a native teacher, a *shaykh*, a Muslim at heart.

His work on al-Hallaj is the major fruit of his investigations, and it is perhaps appropriate for me, its English translator, to comment on it in this context.

2

It is, first of all, a work that employed most fully all of Massignon's gifts and techniques of investigation. While in the form of meticulous research, it is nevertheless a work that could not have been undertaken and sustained, except on a very small and pedantic scale, without Massignon's profound belief in the authenticity and originality of its subject. In fact, without some comparable belief, few Westerners beyond those drawn to contemporary strategic policy studies, pure pedants, transcendental ecumenicists, crackpot adventurers, literary fantasists, or religious missionaries have been aroused to study Islam at all. Al-Hallaj was more to Massignon than the subject of a doctoral dissertation and he seemed to represent no threat to the security of modern France. He was a living (not to be read ethereally as a "timeless") person whose civilization also came to life with him, and from the moment of their first encounter until his death, Massignon devoted his gifts, energy, and personal resources to the presentation of this other's life. To some political opponents the other absorbed him so deeply that through him the radical al-Hallaj did eventually become an enemy of France and of the authority of the church.

Always putting aside any such considerations, he began to publish the first outlines of his work in 1909 and thereafter appeared a series of expanded versions and relevant editions of supportive texts. The process was interrupted before the Great War, and then resumed in 1919, culminating in its presentation in two volumes as his doctoral *thèse principale* in 1922. It was the publication of this work plus that of his critically important *thèse complèmentaire*, his famous *Essai* on the origins of the technical vocabulary of Islamic mysticism, that fulfilled his earlier promise and recognition as a genius. While many believe this first edition to be the more eloquent and definitive of the two editions,* he considered it incomplete and not ready for translation or wider dissemination when Mary Mellon first approached him at Ascona in 1939. He devoted the period of 1922–1962 to its completion, with the final task of editing left to his surviving son and daughter, to two Arabist colleagues, Henri Laoust and Louis Gardet, and, as it so happened, to me. The work is now available to be examined with my accompanying biographical introduction to Massignon himself. The present book, I feel certain, represents the last time I shall dare to intrude upon the life of one who shied even from having his photograph taken; and it is not a biography but a memoir with these few strokes of commentary. The one he felt was to be made known was al-Hallaj, not himself. And he hoped new studies of al-Hallaj would succeed his own.

---

*La Passion d'al-Hallaj, 1st ed., 2 vols. (Paris: Geuthner, 1922); 2nd ed., 4 vols. (Paris: Gallimard, 1975).

To know al-Hallaj as Massignon knew him, we must keep in mind the latter's particular gifts and inclinations, notably his concern with Semitism: with Arabic language, with texts, with Qur'an, with traditions, with Sacred Law. He believed in the Qur'anic opening to Christ—or what Seyyed Hossein Nasr has called the "Christic" dimension of the Qur'an, comparable to its "Judaic" and "Islamic" dimensions—with whose martyrdom al-Hallaj identified his own.* This was the source of the Persian al-Hallaj's own Semitism and of his own acceptance of its spiritual language and its laws to the very end. He was influenced by the Hellenism dominant in the intellectual circles of his day, but to Massignon he was not inspired by it and, in many respects, stood in opposition to the aestheticism and neo-gnosticism of its Muslim literary and philosophical exponents gathered in the Baghdad of his day (the late tenth century A.D.). Al-Hallaj's insistence on bearing witness publicly to one's love of God and to the teachings and law of God, even at the cost of one's own life, separated him from both the more worldly wise and prudent as well as the more esoteric Hellenists.

In many ways, as historians of early Islam can readily perceive, the opposition between the philosophical Hellenists and the Qur'an-based traditionalists in al-Hallaj's time was not new. It represented a further stage in the characteristic and ongoing internal tension of Islam that began following the Prophet Muhammad's death (in 632 A.D.), when the Arab tribes encountered Zoroastrian Iran and Byzantine Christian Syria and Egypt. The tension reached its first dramatic intellectual clarification with the

---

Presence de Louis Massignon, Hommages et témoignages (Paris, 1987), p. 51.

establishment in the early 800s by the half-Persian Hellenist Caliph al-Ma'mum of the celebrated translation center, *Bait al-Hikma* ("the House of Wisdom") in the recently created (in 762 A.D.) and increasingly cosmopolitan city of Baghdad. It was the feverish activity of translation, primarily of Greek learning into Arabic, that led to the permanent clash in Islam between the speculative philosophers and the old entrenched apologists for the primacy of the Qur'an and its literal acceptance by Muslims. This fever culminated in the Hellenists' unprecedented creation of an inquisitional court to impose a new orthodoxy on the community and the traditionalists' subsequent use of the court to rid the community of the speculatists once their political power was broken. Al-Hallaj's execution, in many ways, stands as a further stage in that ongoing crisis that continues today in a struggle between the Qur'anic revivalists and those open to foreign influences, both arguing from contrary premises for the renewal of Islamic society. Most Westerners, out of self-interest, tend to simplify the opposition as between the good, open-minded, speculative, outward-looking liberal thinkers and the bad, closed-minded, dogged adherents to tradition and conformism. Massignon's reading was not so simplified.

First, he noted that the ultra-traditionalist Hanbalite school, which was responsible in Iraq for, among other things, the rote teaching of the Qur'an to the young, included the staunchest defenders of al-Hallaj, the supposed radical revolutionary and crypto-anthropomorphist heretic. Further, he found al-Hallaj's perception of the true condition of his times (858 to 922 A.D.) drawn like that of many of the traditionalists from the plight of its victims. The blacks and bedouins were the despised and

23

exploited, and al-Hallaj was outspoken on behalf of both. Through his gradual discovery of the sources of their exploitation, he perceived that the community of Islam itself was the victim—not of philosophic Hellenism surely, but of the simple greed and self-indulgence of public officials, judges, lawyers, bankers, and more mundane speculators and betrayers of the community's resources and the public trust. This dichotomy of the few elite wealthy versus the many poor was unjust according to the teachings of the Qur'an, but was accommodated by the community's growing passivity. As the late Egyptian poet Salah 'Abd al-Sabur* dramatized in his 1965 play *Ma'sat al-Hallaj* ("The Tragedy of al-Hallaj"), Hallaj was an awakener of his community by the call to justice and truth, the *sayha bi'l-Haqq*, and he died a martyr, according to this modern poet, for that genuinely Islamic cause. While this is certainly a dimension of al-Hallaj's story, noted fully by Massignon in his magnum opus, the story is also more complex.

The Hellenists undoubtedly benefited from the patronage of the "bankers" and contributed to the cultural efflorescence of the age. They also, like the traditionalists, had to safeguard and enhance their own position of intellectual leadership in the community. The majority of both camps, in this regard, were united in assuming the position of prudence against the growing public unrest that attended the person and preaching of al-Hallaj and his cry for "Truth" (one of the Qur'anic Holy Names for God). Furthermore, the majority of both groups could unite in opposition to one of his alleged utterances, which he himself did not deny, the famous *Anâ'l-Haqq* (literally

---

*Died August 15, 1981.

"I am the truth" or figuratively "God is in me as the Truth"). They could do so on Qur'anic grounds, specifically condemning the identifying of any *thing*, including oneself, with God; and on neo-gnostic grounds, opposing the notion of the transcendent God's being accessible to lowly and impure man. Al-Hallaj violated, it would seem, both Semitism and Hellenism, and he was proclaimed by scholars and public officials a *zindiq* (a "heretic," a dualist) guilty of *shirk* ("associationism," idolatry) and of preaching the breaking of the Sacred Law that calls for the duty of pilgrimage to Mecca (when he, a three-time pilgrim to the Holy City, spoke of the spiritual efficacy and legitimacy of symbolic pilgrimage in one's own home). It was judged lawful by a court of eighty-four legal signatories to spill his blood. He himself believed he was uniting his beloved God and His community of Muslims against himself and thereby bore witness *in extremis* to the *tawhīd* (the "oneness") of both. He was castigated by many as a crypto-Christian for "distorting" the monotheistic revelation "in the Christian way," and he called upon Jesus in his suffering. To Massignon, al-Hallaj was first and last a Muslim, and a witness of the Qur'an's spiritual treasury of inspiration.

To Massignon the experience of al-Hallaj's union with *al-Haqq* had been "real," not theoretical, and for that reason had been impossible to contain through prudence. He and even his more timorous disciples believed he had been singled out by God for special (not esoteric) conversation with Himself and humiliation in public. Massignon believed that this conversation (*shath*) was the essential oddity and uniqueness of al-Hallaj's position in the history of Islamic mysticism: the personal exchange of words and in public. He and God spoke together, so much so that al-Hallaj was considered mad by many but listened to by many more, especially by both the traditionally educated and the common people, as well as by some of the curious elite, whose true conditions and hearts he "read." He spoke of his "Beloved," his "Friend," "You," as filling him with His presence to the point where his only self was Himself and he could no longer even remember his own name. For such utterances and those other indiscretions for justice, he was pursued by the authorities, who cited the danger to law and order and imprisoned him. Through the intervention of certain of his disciples in high places, including the current caliph's own mother, he was kept in prison rather than executed. But the postponement ended after nine years, when their support was weakened by even less favorable political conditions, and he was finally put to death March 26, 922.

Massignon, struck deeply in 1907 by the accounts of al-Hallaj's death, set himself the task of understanding the man and the civilization in which such a story occurred. It was a story not unfamiliar in the West, where accounts of the martyrdom of Joan of Arc, of Sir Thomas More, or indeed of Socrates in Athens, and of Jesus in Jerusalem were constantly retold. But Islam has few such examples. Massignon's sense of "correspondences" seized him. He was himself at the time non-religious, certainly a non-practitioner of any religion. His initial inquiries were therefore not religiously and certainly not ecumenically motivated. The "correspondence" aspect, which appears undeniably in his 1922 edition of *La Passion d'al-Hallaj*, became crystalized religiously only after a dramatic experience of his own in May of 1908 during an archaeological "mission en Mesopotamie"* when he was cap-

---

*His own account was published under this title, vol. I, Cairo, 1910; vol. II, Cairo, 1912, by Institut Français d'Archéologie Orientale.

tured by Turkish soldiers on suspicion of spying for the French. He was imprisoned, sick with malaria, and attempted to take his own life, an act thwarted, he believed, by an intervention of God. It is a subject of which he spoke often and in public and which I include in the "diary" portion of this book. Whatever the nature of this experience, Massignon subsequently combined his powerful scholarly gifts with an equally powerful belief in the Unique, Transcendent, and Absolute God. Muslims consider his "conversion" an authentic testimony of Islam.

3

Setting aside his twelve books on Islamic studies and editions of Arabic texts, a careful reading of the three volumes of Massignon's *Opera minora* and the selected essays of *Parole donnée* reveals not only the startling range of his subjects but also the specific depth of his religious vocations in Roman Catholicism.

Just as there are many dimensions to Massignon the Islamist, of which I have shown but a few here, so are there many dimensions to Massignon the Roman Catholic, of which I shall explore a few now, hoping my remarks may direct readers to a fuller examination of his thought through his own works.

Those close to the family insist that the earliest and foremost religious influence on Louis was his mother, Marie Hovyn Massignon, and what he described to me as her "secret practice of her faith." His father, Fernand Massignon, a physician as well as a painter and sculptor known by the pseudonym of "Pierre Roche," was a skeptic and preferred his son to be raised the same.* Louis's mother's faith was traditionally Catholic. Her very deep prayer life contained a special devotion to the Virgin Mary.

His father's only Christian friend was the novelist and Catholic convert Joris Karl Huysmans. Though I have written elsewhere in the Foreword to the English edition of the *Passion* [xxv-xxvii] of the varied influence of Huysmans' writing and thought upon Louis, it is appropriate to concentrate further in this context on one aspect of it: his view of substitutive suffering, which is an essential part of Louis's faith and also of his understanding of al-Hallaj's acceptance of martyrdom. The two Christian themes that early on attracted Louis Massignon were reverence for the Virgin Mary and belief in the spiritual power of suffering. Though they both assume the form of doctrines in many believing minds, Louis approached them concretely and experientially at their sources, not through dogmatic formulations. The Virgin Mary is the Semitic mother of Jesus, the emblem of humility and purity in the Gospels and in the Qur'an; and while ignoring the preference of many ecclesiastics for her assumption and glory, Massignon nevertheless, through his own reverential process of glorification, transformed her into a symbolic prism reflecting the hearts of all women, whom he believed to retain virginal centers regardless of their exploitations and violations by men.

---

*Pierre Roche" was active in the Societé des Droits de l'Homme with Emile Zola, was of the left and against the church but liberal, that is, against its destruction, and was also a supporter of the Impressionists along with Joris Karl Huysmans. His son derived from him a deep belief in "the integrity of ideas."

In regard to his celebrated chivalric respect for women he was considered by many to be quaint. But this respect accounts for his body of writing on women and the "correspondences" with the Virgin he found in such disparate figures as Fatima, the daughter of the Prophet Muhammad, and Marie Antoinette, the martyred Queen of France. His interest in Fatima yielded more fruitful results for scholarship, especially as it led him to a deeper appreciation of the Muslim Shi'ite tradition both in its reverence for the Prophet's family and, through its ritualization of the martyrdom of Muhammad's grandson Husayn, in its concern with the value of suffering. To some these interests were marginal and eccentric. To the indefatigable investigative Massignon what was eccentric or irrelevant to one man was another's passage to discoveries and illuminations. The result, in his written work, is often a network of multi-channeled pursuits which make sense only at the end, when the whole is apparent.

Massignon was always fascinated with beginnings, with roots. The roots of Christianity were found in the Virgin's humility, in the presence of the divine *fiat*, in her patient fidelity to her vow, and in the fruit of her womb, her child, the human person and the martyr Jesus, whom a woman, Mary Magdalen, was chosen to witness first as the resurrected Christ Who through His suffering at the hands of men had ended substitutively and for all time humanity's enslavement to sin and death.

Huysmans, the sophisticated author of "the first decadent novel" *A rebours* (translated in various English editions as *Against Nature* or *Against the Grain*), noted for his self-absorption rather than simple faith or sincerity, underwent a conversion and then immersed himself in piety. This culminated in his hagiographical study* of Blessed Lydwine of Schiedam, a little-known Dutch saint of the early fifteenth century, with whose physical sufferings he identified his own cancer of the throat and who, he believed, transferred mystically to him through *substitution* the spiritual power to reach "a level beyond" the self that enabled him to endure and find more than mere intellectual meaning—indeed, salvation—in his own suffering. The idea of mystical substitution was studied thoroughly by Massignon in his investigations of al-Hallaj, for whom he always regarded Huysmans a corresponding source of understanding.

Despite Massignon's exhaustive explanations of the mystical substitution "thesis," there are reviewers who quite reasonably dismiss the idea and call the explanations inadequate. It is one instance in which sources do not guarantee understanding. The notion of mystical substitution, by its very nature, can only be rooted in experience, not explanation, and is verifiable even then only at the extremes of personal suffering when rationality, as normally understood, ceases to be definitive as a guide. For this reason Massignon himself wanted always, in every aspect of his life and work, to go as far as possible "to the limit," as one of his most penetrating and personal essays is entitled.** He did not accept secondary source information any more than would his most serious critics, and he expected them to question and, if appro-

---

*Reprinted in English translation by Tan Books and Publishers, Inc., Rockford, Ill. 1979.

**Included in *Parole donnée*, ed. V. Monteil (Paris: Julliard, 1962).

priate, amend his readings of primary sources. But as a person of relentless self-discipline and physical prowess who enjoyed excellent health throughout his life, he did not until the very end—and then he communicated nothing about it—experience the limit of physical suffering unto death.

For this "failure," as he often put it, he felt a curious guilt. A Muslim colleague who enjoyed playing devil's advocate reminded him on occasion that he would not die a martyr's death like Jesus or al-Hallaj. On an unusual level it was the familiar problem of researching, feeling, and even understanding without being chosen to actually do: the scholar's paradox, one that gave him "spiritual worry" throughout his life. More timid or prudent—most would say, wiser—scholars never know this worry. But Massignon was by nature a risk-taker, and following his own "conversion," he became by belief a Christian risk-taker. It was unquestionably through al-Hallaj that he was "reminded" of his religious roots and by whom he was turned back to discover, as if for the first time, his French and Catholic origins.

In both al-Hallaj's and Christian testimonies, as he believed, *substitution* is not willed by the receiver of its power. Rather, in suffering one is moving paradoxically through an act of suspension of personal will, in the recognition of its limitation for achieving what it ultimately seeks: the end of suffering—and eternal life. One wills nothing but rather surrenders everything, through utter nakedness of self and soul and awaits the unexpected, the gratuitous, the mysterious power beyond the will. One moves to the desert to offer one's nakedness, however, not to test the existence of the gratuitous. And there, if one's suffering is real and one is sincere, it ap-

31

pears; but even then only to a very few "witnesses" or "substitutes" (in Arabic *abdāl*), to a spiritual "elite," through whom substitution is the raising to another level of the soul by the power of the source of grace.

The danger to the human self from such a notion would seem to be the subtle cultivation of spiritual arrogance on the one hand, of passivity and dependence on the other. In the hyper-intelligent as well as self-willed, action-oriented Massignon, his friend Charles de Foucauld, the tireless self-analyzing and self-documenting Huysmans, or indeed the ceaselessly journeying abroad al-Hallaj, the danger was the first not the second of these commonest of civilization's malaises. Each in his own way "wrestled with the angel," each was a witness on the frontier of experience, and each became sources for others, like the sources whose intimacy they knew themselves. They believed that substitution was efficacious as a homeopathic process of renewal extending from person to person, beginning from God to humanity, and was likened to the process of faith itself extending to unite members of a community in the belief in One Source of all things. The process of substitution extended through an elite of chosen individuals across time, infusing into the larger community through their "life sufferings" the restorative power of grace and thereby renewal of faith. Identification of these individuals was the crux of Massignon's post-conversion research and the source of much scholarly criticism raised against him. Indeed, he spoke unabashedly on occasion of being a donkey carrying the relics of those "who made it," particularly Huysmans, Foucauld, the Jewish convert nun Violet Sussman, and al-Hallaj. What he meant was that he thought each of these had attained the first stage of authentic nakedness of self and soul, and had left to him to carry to others relics that testified to the efficacy of mystical substitution. He never believed he himself was "a substitute" or that he had known more than "a hint" of the divine source.

He made pious visitations to numerous saints' tombs, both Islamic and Christian, and to sites holy to Judaism, Hinduism, Buddism, and Shintoism,* noting each in his letters to friends and in his penetrating articles mislabelled by his editors "minor" works. The sheer physical effort of going from place to place around the globe, employing every and any means from airplane to burro to get to them, is unimaginable to most of us. Yet he had both energy and interest in learning from others whom he met of the usually more modest routes they had taken, in which he was able to see astonishing connections and significances unknown to themselves.

Unlike the traditional English parodies of lofty encyclopedic minds, Massignon's mind was never boring; if he frequently exhausted his listeners, he did so while keeping them thoroughly awake. His expectation, I believe, was that they shared at some level his enthusiasm for even the smallest of life's details, not that they believed everything he said.

He had a rare devotion to relics, as his acquaintances knew. He kept several in his study among his books and papers, and the combination conveyed the atmosphere of ongoing investigation and, from a distance, of imaginative confusion. There were relics of places and persons unfamiliar to me when I met him, of La Salette, of Catherine Emmerich, of Soeur Mélanie, to mention but

---

*Note especially the remarkable 1960 account "Meditations d'un passant aux bois sacrées d'Isé," included in *Parole donnée*.

three of the striking ones he carried emblematically on or around his person. He had, like Huysmans, the European fascination with holy bones and hair and the like, not shared by most Muslims or Americans. In fact, he is, despite his rare breadth of experience beyond Europe, only explicable dressed in his black academic suit, seated in his particular French cultural context, which seemed at times an expression of conscious archaism, though never offered by him without a wink or an ironic smile. Yet having said this, I realize he is also not explicable outside the context of his Arabic text-lined shelves in his Cairo study circa 1912, attired in his black wool jalaba, or traveling at a fast pace through oases and covered markets pursuing evidence of spiritual and human value between and beyond both worlds.

He also had an exceptional knowledge of the rituals of his own and other religions. Memory served him admirably in this realm, too. There is a story of his being on a Turkish ship on the Sea of Marmara, just prior to World War I, when death struck one of the crew members, a Muslim. The captain and crew knew nothing of the proper ritual prayers to offer for the dead man prior to burial at sea, yet felt obliged to inquire among the passengers to see if anyone knew. Only one young Frenchman traveling to Istanbul knew them and performed them reverently.

His yearly visits to Jerusalem, with his pious recitation from memory of the one hundred and fifty psalms at the Wailing Wall and his lying stretched out on the floor in extended prayer inside the Holy Sepulchre, were recorded by many eyewitnesses despite his effort at privacy. His capacity for prayers was as enormous as his capacity for words.

One of Massignon's secrets in collecting relics, making pious visitations, and communicating his findings and experience to students, colleagues, friends, enemies, and anonymous audiences, was his ability to concentrate himself in the immediate present into which he brought his many encounters from the past. He always listened in the present or at least seemed to by the evidence of his attentiveness and responses. He never looked at his watch for verification or prompting or escape. Indeed, he believed time was another subject for investigation whose primary source readers were not the grand philosophers such as Kant or Hegel, but physicians who took pulses and knew, as did mediaeval Muslim physicians, the circulation of the blood, or dancers and poets who knew rhythm and meter. And he wrote of mystics, both Christian and Muslim, whose sense of time was in "instants," "divine touches," or what Joyce, his natural correspondent in fiction, whom he quoted on occasion, called "epiphanous moments" and Eliot "still points" that formed "a constellation" (which the latter in his *Four Quartets* made almost a cliché among the learned) of experimental *wujūd* or "ecstatic moments" extending and altering our consciousness of time beyond our sense of its merely being the fourth dimension of space in an expanding universe.* He was intensely interested in modern science, perhaps more than in modern literature, and accepted proudly the tutoring given him by his physicist son Daniel, for he believed science more than literature revealed the nature of things and clarified knowledge. But he was vigilant as to the fictionalizing by scientists

---

*See "Le Temps dans la pensée islamique," included in *Parole donnée*.

35

as well, especially in their presumptive hypotheses that often exceeded their evidence. He rejected both poets and scientists as prophets, excluding them from what he considered a more seminal and selfless calling. But he believed that the progress of science was in closer correspondence with the progress of religious wisdom and served it ultimately better than did literature. I came to him believing the opposite.*

His various positions and themes were arrived at systematically but also idiosyncratically. His Catholic friends who recognized him as a "genius" with "esoteric sources" and a spiritual brother following his conversion that was matched by theirs—I refer principally to his contemporary friends, Maritain, Claudel, Chardin, Marcel, Mauriac, and Bernanos, and the somewhat younger Jean Daniélou, to mention just a few—all belonged to the modern French Catholic renascence and all in their various individual ways produced its interesting diversity. He wrote volumes of letters to them all as well as to many non- or

---

*Our difference in this respect was not absolute, but reflected entirely historical developments and cultural changes affecting our different periods of formation. As a young man in the late nineteenth century he had been exposed thoroughly to the decadence and shallow aetheticism of the Parisian litterati. In the mid-twentieth century my contemporaries had all been exposed thoroughly to the arrogant elitism and self-indulgence of scientism of American academic circles. Literary people, even the ubiquitous critics, were no longer celebrated or important enough to be considered either culturally beneficial or threatening. I was therefore more hopeful about writers whose abuses of power didn't affect anyone, and less so about scientists, who were, after all, the mandarins of destruction in every post World War II person's youth. It was an inevitable difference of context, experience, and time that made us both insist all the more on simplicity, at least of language, in our communications.

anti-Catholic thinkers and writers, some of which have begun to be published in separate volumes.* But one of the few whose works he actually quoted was the radical Catholic novelist Léon Bloy, whose interest in the Jewish origins of Christianity corresponded to his own and whose sense of the poor and the despised exceeded his knowledge and informed him. Massignon enjoyed, like Gide, needling Claudel for his missionary zeal and pomposity, but he also quoted his views frequently and chose him as his daughter Geneviève's godfather. The one who clearly held his deepest affection was Jacques Maritain, who he believed was a saint, but he didn't identify with Maritain's thought beyond the level of appreciation. He was no more a Thomist than he was a writer of fiction, and somehow in his mind the two were assigned approximately the same place in importance. In his view none of the Catholic writers prior to or during his time—that is, in late nineteenth- and twentieth-century France—exceeded or went to the limits of existing knowledge, except Huysmans on the mystical level, and Bloy on the radical Christian level.** The others were admirable but essentially reseeded and harvested the old ground of Catholic subject material and thought. Chardin and Daniélou, both of whose scientific expertise he respected, were not especially convincing as visionaries or historians of God's plan, their work being too theoretical in sum-

---

*Note especially *Claudel et Massignon*, ed. M. Malicet (Paris, 1973); *Max Van Berchem et Louis Massignon*, ed. W. Vycichl (Leiden, 1980); and *Charles de Foucauld* by Denise and Robert Barrat (Paris, 1958).

**To these he added Charles de Foucauld. These three "in their return to God, were distinguished by a discipline of fasting and prayer." *Parole donnée*, p. 277.

mary to intrigue him even in the realm of ideas. To a great extent he stood apart as "a Catholic thinker" and almost cannot be called one, certainly not in any conventional or parochial sense. Yet of all the aforementioned he was the only one whose "vocation," not resolved at an early time by "conversion," evolved further as "a curve" through a surprising and seemingly endless series of turns and twists, culminating at the end in priesthood.* He was the only one who remained elusive and unpredictable, virtually religiously "free," yet bound to his sources.

As has been noted, he was equally at home among Muslims as among Catholics, respecting and to some extent practicing the rituals of each. His religious consciousness was rooted in ritual, not in theological speculation, dogma, or world-building. However, on the Islamic side, while he was most learned and affirmative of Islam's Arabic and Sunni ritual and traditional orthodoxy (he often said "one must be orthodox, of course"), he was more than a little open to Iranian Shi'ite ritual and mystical heterodoxy and was a pathfinder by his research in the latter as he was in the former. Similarly, in Christianity, while being "orthodox," he was nevertheless drawn increasingly in his later years to certain positions taken by Christian sects, notably to those of the traditional "peace sects" on the power of non-violent action and resistance, which corresponded to the views of Gandhi. He measured sectarian positions carefully against orthodoxy's responses, however, just as he measured radical stances on justice against respect for law. One of his most consistent underlying arguments, presented in his monthly "bulletins" of the *Amis de Gandhi* and *Badaliya*

---

*Daniélou was, of course, like Chardin, a Jesuit and was, finally, a Cardinal of the Church.

sodalities, and aimed at the members of each, was one informed by both al-Hallaj's and Catholic tradition's acceptance of law; namely, that change could be brought about most creatively and effectively when those seeking it for just reasons recognized three things first before assuming positions of concerted action: (1) the sources of possible injustice in themselves, (2) the humanity of their opponents, (3) the real state of things existing then as distinguished from the state their dreams hoped to bring about. If such were fully recognized, erroneous enthusiasms and faulty thinking could be challenged from within rather than demolished, along with the good intent, from without. By such circumspection one's cause itself could be clarified, articulated, and fought for more persuasively. But he also realized that opportunities for circumspection could run out and opposition could be immovable. In one such bulletin he wrote a passage which needs to be cited at length:*

In bulletin number 10, we recalled the profound words of Pascal on "the long strange war" that violence wages against truth. "All efforts of violence cannot enfeeble the truth nor serve any other purpose than to heighten it. And all the lights of truth can do nothing to stop violence and only serve to irritate it further." (*Prov. Lett.* XII)

We have not hesitated to witness in public, before law courts and even in the streets, in silence and non-violence, against official illegalities, especially regarding the many crimes committed against Muslims. In this contradictory age, of the "possessed," which we are passing through, I can only echo Pascal that the affirmation of truth, even in non-

---

*My translation published by Dorothy Day in *The Catholic Worker*, November 1961.

violence, serves only to irritate our blinded adversaries and to render them even worse (as for the victims, they consider us lukewarm). What we wish is not to bring on reprisals by enflaming the victims to vengeance, but to convert the persecutors, who are also our brothers.

Why this apparent flaw in non-violence for witnessing truth (and, what is indispensable, all truth)? Gandhi explained it by observing that a brutal witnessing in favor of truth, using apparent physical non-violence, opens the way to a spiritual violence, to a weapon more menacing than the worst material weapons. When we use truth as a privilege and monopoly to force an adversary to humiliate himself as a liar, then the flickering conscience which he has even in his most indefensible physical violences is unable to submit to our truth, because we have refused to recognize that he has a conscience at all.

The desire for martyrdom (the danger of pride in noble souls) discloses through physical non-violence a spiritual violence that wishes to wound the soul of the sinner while breaking his sin.

What can we therefore do when the menace of civil war (and even religious war, due to the blind hatred of certain missionaries who are writing against "the Mohammedan imposter allied to communism") threatens us more and more in both France and Algeria.

We must be more meek and humble in defending the truth when we are called to do so. (What is more disarming and persuasive than the humility of a living crucifix?) We must not defend the truth as a personal possession, but agree to be wounded for it, and even by it, just as our dissenting brothers are: for we wish to die accursed for our brothers who are lost. And we do not wish our country torn in two by civil war.

The time has passed for recourse to legal justice as a means of settling a conflict as profound as this between our brothers of both sides. In the community life that Charles de Foucauld envisioned (*Directoire*, 3rd ed., Paris, 1961, p. 65.) there is this: All those who hate evil will love men. They will be *universal saviours*. They will avoid legal trials, not debating before courts, surrendering their rights rather than disputing them, "accepting humiliation."

There is no other way for truth to overcome violence.

Only Massignon among his distinguished friends was prepared to go to the political limits, to take to the streets, yet only as a man who respected law more deeply than did those officials betraying its trust, not as a political insurgent. If the law arrested him, he obeyed. If it put him to death, he hoped he would accept like al-Hallaj its rightness. Though he was mercifully not pressed to the limit, despite physical attacks on his person during the Algerian war years, one made by a fellow Catholic who struck him on the head with a chair while he was delivering a talk at the Centre Universitaire des Intellectuels Catholiques (in 1958), he was prepared to accept it if indicated. It should be added, of course, that he, among all his Catholic friends, was the only one who had some official government status (he carried an ambassador-at-large passport throughout his life, following World War I), and this made him a public figure, as the others (except for Claudel, who served terms as Ambassador to the United States and to Japan) were not. Such status also gave him free passage on airplanes flying abroad, which accounted for the vast travel possibilities open to him.

If his Catholicism was orthodox and law-abiding (obedient to church and respectful to state), it was also direct and radical in its criticism of unjust social conditions and the abuses of power that created injustices. This apparent dichotomy has since his time become easier (at least theoretically) to unify in thought and action and indeed

41

more commonplace as a phenomenon even among the clergy. Mention nowadays of all these *themes* and *positions* is hardly news. Yet in Massignon the tension between the two moved him into "actions" and he made news. What was not expected, even by his friends, though it should have been, was the further turns of his Catholic vocation. First, he became a Franciscan tertiary, which was hardly scandalous; and second, he became a priest in the Melikite rite and offered mass in Arabic according to the Greek liturgy of St. John Chrysostom (circa 347 to 407) at the Church of St. Julien le Pauvre in Paris on special occasions though regularly in a chapel created in his own home and attended by communicants. He seldom spoke of his priesthood and then only prudently. It was only by rare and special dispensation directly from the conservative Pope Pius XII that such ordination had been possible.

His priesthood was a fact difficult for many to accept or understand, yet it became the spiritual mainstay of the last period of his life. Without it, I am sure, he could not have found the strength and resourcefulness to endure what he had to undergo during France's "fratricidal war" in Algeria. This period was in numerous ways the climax of his life as an Islamicist and as a Frenchman, as one whose two sides were divided violently against themselves. He was perceived by many as one in whom the drama was most intensely contained and in whom both nations' terror and pity for suffering humankind could find its most resounding cries for sanity and mercy. He surrendered himself wholly to those cries and by the war's termination in mid-1962 he was exhausted and within a few months died.

Without exploring his Catholicism further, a task for

others than myself who knew it in him as a living, animating, and evocative source, not as a subject for study, I would be remiss if I did not acknowledge what may be its most important legacy for others now or in the future: its ecumenical dimension, which was founded solidly on his belief in the authenticity of Islam and on his own participative evolution as a Christian, both the result of experiential knowledge and ritual practice. Pope John XXIII "blessed" his vocation to the priesthood and also "blessed" the Muslim-Christian pilgrimage at the Seven Sleepers shrine in Vieux Marché, Bretagne, which he had helped organize. This witnessing of fraternity in time of war Massignon believed was his most important work as a Christian. His "dialogue" was built from real walls and windows and with respect for each one's architecture of belief and devotion. It was never formless or sentimental. At that time it was undertaken with considerable risk—to him, his family, the Muslims, the Christians, the Bretons, and the foreigners who participated. All who celebrated with him the rite of hospitality, "the rite of Abraham" as he called the rituals and the spiritual friendship, accepted the risk with which the atmosphere was charged. The fruit of the reunion each year, from 1954 until his death in 1962 and all the years following to the present, has been that of continuing and new friendships entered into without fear of risks. Along with his scholarship, this spiritual reunion remains his legacy.

4

One of Massignon's dominant themes, both in his Christian and in his Islamic work, is that of *friendship*.

Like *mystical substitution*, it had its origins in early experience. Suffice it to say that his boyhood and school friendships were deep, intense, and demanding. The closest, into his early twenties, were those with Henri Maspero, Paul Kraus, and a Spanish grandee, the first two sharing his scholarly interests and the latter two his travels. They were each tirelessly inquisitive, voluminous readers, and enthusiastic sharers of ideas and experiences. Henri's father, the Egyptologist Gaston Maspero, was especially generous with the use of his library for the two friends, and it was there no doubt that both of their interests in the Orient were stirred. The demands of one friend upon the other, in the cases of the Spaniard and of Kraus, reached the intensity of love. Their premature deaths were referred to on several occasions by Massignon to the end of his life.

He himself could be very demanding, seductive, and controlling of friends. He was never neutral about anything and was often, no doubt also as a parent, overwhelming. He was a large presence whom one could not ignore or resist or at times escape. At times he was too large. His presence, learning, and courage fostered in some dependence and discipleship. In this his greatest human-relational capacity he was himself most vulnerable and capable of self-deception. Often he was disappointed and hurt by friends, especially in the latter period of his life when he thought they failed him through their lack of courage to support his humanitarian causes.

He felt the pain of increasing solitude in old age and feared the diminution of his powers and interest to others. He was human and his latent human feelings bothered him deeply. He struggled visibly against his own attractions, suspicions, and rages, at times without success.

If unleashed, his temper could be as fearsome as his courtesy could be gentle. He seemed to many an outrageous clash of contradictory states. Nothing about him was lukewarm and nothing he did was in halves. He was at times excessively trusting and gullible. At others, impatient and judgmental. All of these states were known by his family and his friends. Officialdom and the public encountered both his wrath and his self-control, prudence, and moral insightfulness. In 1983 at the time of the national commemoration of the centenary of his birth, the dignitaries of the church, state, university, and French Academy preferred to enshrine a benign official Massignon. The veiling of his complex personal characteristics, however, meant the loss of an important ingredient in his thought: the meaning of *friendship.*

To Massignon the word was many-layered and had evolved those layers over a long period of time, not merely the period of his own lifetime. Friendship was not merely the naming of boyhood and adult friends with whom he intimately shared the world; it was a way of life and a worldview. It began not with the shy Henri in the lycées Montaigne and Louis-le-Grand but with the sources they both found there. It was particularly Massignon's predisposition for friendship that found in the sources a world of interlacing itineraries beginning as far back as the tales of Gilgamesh and Enkidu, of Achilles and Patroclus; it was assimilated in the medieval tales of the knights errant, the accounts of Roland and Oliver, of Amis and Amile, and echoed in the Franciscan order of mendicant Friars and in the Islamic mystical orders of brotherhoods; all were based on belief in the vow and perpetuated through spiritual values of bravery, fidelity, and honor. A further dimension of Massignon's thought was thus mythic, grounded in ancient pre-monotheistic wisdom and fable. There were aspects even of his appearance that, if prophetic in message and tone, seemed older, more primitive than biblical, more of the angry and downcast Utnapishtim's spirit than that of Noah or Abraham, yet anticipating the latter's devotion and readiness to sacrifice to the Lord.

His instinct for the presence of holy places, like that for discovering hidden texts, was more of a diviner's or a sorcerer's gift than a modern academic scholar's, and his power to evoke the story of each one's origins and to revive the lost or forgotten ritual, locate the abandoned site, and read the revealing passage, as if he were himself personally its old interpreter restored momentarily to life, carried in itself the aura of ageless mystery. In his hands each ritual or passage seemed incredibly old, yet alive and speaking the language of today. His sense of the global and the ecumenical was organic rather than transcendental. Such transcendent meaning as there may be in each had a beginning and was therefore to be found implanted in the earth. The source was a hidden spring to be divined and drunk from, as the desert nomad drinks from his well.

It was this organic sense of the "desert" that motivated the Irish monks, whom he admired, to build their hermitages in crags on uninhabited islands overlooking the sea and Foucauld to "disappear" on the Moroccan wastelands in God. That was the divined "communion," the true source of "dialogue," the "meaning" of pilgrimage. And the Seven Sleepers of Ephesus, especially with its Qur'anic concept of *futuwwa* or spiritual brotherhood calling for the surrender, the *islam*, of its members' individual wills in obedience to the Merciful and the Compassionate God and thereby destroying the idols of themselves—

calling, that is, for them to "sleep" in the cave—formed in his mind the quintessential fusion of myth and doctrine centered on the notion of human friendship and the friendship between God and men. Preserved as a didactic tale in the *Legenda Aurea* of the thirteenth-century Italian hagiographer Jacobus de Voragine, as well as in the Qur'an, it was also found to exist in the Breton *Gwerz* literature accounts of the founding of the chapel at Vieux Marché on the site of a Dolmen crypt, and it had been spread by similar fusions through other parts of Europe, North Africa, and the Near East to various "divined" sites. Such a site was located by him in his ancestral Brittany as the fitting place for the fraternal Muslim-Christian pilgrimage in 1954. His curiously gathered knowledge revealed itself of a piece in the continuing "curve" of his life.

Furthermore, the focus of al-Hallaj's mystical love poetry was centered on the lover's relationship with his beloved Friend, which was the highest expression Massignon knew by any poet of this theme of friendship. As such it pointed him also to a deeper understanding of Jesus Christ, not as the flying superman of Latin church ceilings, but as the intimate and self-abnegating friend of mankind.

The question raised by his continuing "Hellenistic" cultural background, which after all detached him sufficiently to systematically investigate the sources stimulating such curiosity, was whether friendship itself was essential to or obstructing of one's pursuit of personal achievement and intellectual enlightenment. It was supportive but was it fundamental to the realization of one's own true excellence or *arête*? Was it basic to his eloquence, courtesy, generosity, counsel, honor, and power ex-

47

pressed by his early teachers, his peers, and himself? What was the true place of friendship in the overall scheme of things, especially as revealed to a "genius"?

His father wanted him to be an Egyptologist, the favorite adventure for the overeducated and rationalist European intellectual explorer of the late nineteenth century, which combined, as Ancient Egypt was undoubtedly supposed to do for one, the mytho-religious consciousness of oriental romance with scientific inquiry, an acceptable fatalism with a philosophic skepticism. Massignon the son went forth with his reputed "genius" onto the spiritual precipice of a bizarre anthropoidal nihilism, and it was his predisposition for making friends with living people, creatures, nature, sources beyond himself, and for friendship at its highest and most intimate level that kept him on real ground and on his feet. At times, especially after his conversion experience, he may have believed Hellenism was the enemy. He especially scored the neo-gnosticism of later post-Hallajian Islamic mysticism and Christian Deism, or indeed any position that tended to abandon textual tradition and ritual for philosophic speculation, whether transcendentalist, theosophist, materialist, or formalist.

He believed in the present, active, responsive, personal God of wisdom, not in the inaccessible, unresponding, and impersonal Idea of wisdom. The political scenario for al-Hallaj's execution had been conceived and instigated by jurisconsults and mystics of the latter view. Still, like al-Hallaj himself, Massignon was undeniably influenced, culturally at least, by both and understood the language and thought of both. What the neo-gnostic Hellenistic position considered irrelevant was the reality and practice of friendship, the journey of two, not one

48

alone; and it rejected the idea of the accessibility of God Himself to man. The tension was between the "universalizing" Hellenism and the "particularizing" Semitism, once again, to the end of both Massignon's and al-Hallaj's lives. The tension of opposites in each was, of course, crucial to their creativity. Had either strain been isolated within the consciousness of either man, the result would have been clever aestheticism or relentless pedantry.

A text written by al-Hallaj during his long imprisonment, the *Tawasin** or so-called "dialogue with Satan," bears excerpting here as it shows the power and almost thespian detachment of al-Hallaj's mind, yet also his ritual piety and reverent belief. It represents a further correspondence for Massignon's own thought and gradually became indistinguishable from it, especially as regards the dangers of ascetic solitude, spiritual possessiveness, and anti-humanistic affirmations of transcendence.

Properly speaking, al-Hallaj assumes the mask of Satan articulating to God the fallen angel's point of view. He says, by way of introduction, that "there had been no monotheist comparable to Satan among the inhabitants of heaven: the Essence appeared to him in all its purity; he forbade himself out of shyness even to wink at it and began to venerate the Beloved in ascetic solitude.

"He was cursed when he attained absolute aloneness and was challenged when, protesting further, he demanded solitariness.

"God said to him: 'Bow down before Adam.'

---

*Louis Massignon, *The Passion of al-Hallāj: Mystic and Martyr of Islam*, trans. Herbert Mason, Bollingen Series 98, Vol. 3: *The Teaching of al-Hallāj*. Copyright © 1982 by Princeton University Press. Excerpts reprinted with permission of Princeton University Press.

"And he said: 'Not before another than You.'

" 'Even if my curse falls upon you?'

" 'It will not hurt me,' Satan said. 'I refuse your command in order to affirm You in your utmost holiness! I am going mad because of You! What is Adam? Nothing but for You! Who am I then, I Satan, to distinguish him or any creature apart from You? I who want no other way to You than through You Yourself, am I to be a scorned lover? If there had been only a glance between us, it would have been right for me to be proud and angry, but I am he who has known You from before eternity itself; I am worth more than Adam, for I have loved You for the longest time! No one, of any of Your creatures, knowns You better than I! My every intention touches You, Your every intention touches me; both existed before Adam. Whether I bow down before another than You or bow down at all, I must return to my source: You created me of fire, and fire returns to fire, according to a balance and a choice that is Your own.

"There is no longer any estrangement for me since I discovered that reconciliation and estrangement are one and the same. As far as I am concerned, if I am forsaken it is Your abandonment which keeps me company. Besides, how could this abandonment occur, since love always rediscovers its Beloved. Glory be to You! In your providence! In the essence of Your inaccessibility for this pious servant, I myself, who bows down before no other than You!

"What keeps me from bowing down is my fidelity to the Single Adored One. I have to uphold the intention that was uttered first to me. To those who say I have distorted this intention by refusing Your commandment, I say I am not distorted: the consciousness of Your favored

50

creature, even when stricken with deception, remains unchanged. Acquired wisdom continues just as it was when it began, even if the individual who receives it becomes deformed.

"I remember You, even now. Pure thought does not need to remember. By it I am commemorated just as You are commemorated. Your commemoration is mine, mine is Yours. How, remembering both, could we both not be together?

"I serve You more purely, in a more empty moment, in a more glorious commemoration, for I served You absolutely for my own happiness, and now I serve You only for Yours.

"We have both withdrawn desire from everything which defends or preserves. You separated, dazzled, and expelled me so I would not confuse myself with You. You cast me far away from others in my zeal for You alone. You deformed me because I was dazzled. You dazzled me because I was exiled. You exiled me because I was Your servant. You judged me because I was Your companion. You displayed my unworthiness because I praised Your glory. You reduced me to a single garment of a pilgrim because of my flight to You. You forsook me because You revealed Yourself to me. You stripped me naked because You clothed me with foreknowledge of You. You gave me foreknowledge of You. You gave me foreknowledge of You because You distinguished me from others. You distinguished me because You had afflicted my desire with weakness for You Yourself.

"So, I have not sinned, no, not against Your commandment. I have not challenged destiny! And I am not disturbed by any distortion of my form. I preserve my balance through these maxims. Were You to punish me with

51

Your fire for all eternity of eternities, I would not bow down before anyone; I would not humble myself before anything, neither immaterial or material, for I recognize neither father nor son to You. My declaration is sincere. I myself am sincere in love! You Yourself are the cause of my not bowing down, You my inventor! If I had failed You in responding to You with less than total love, I would have been a poor lover. No one loves You more totally than I for Yourself alone. To me You have proven Your uniqueness, to You I have proven my fidelity.' "

Al-Hallaj, in his summary, detaches the mask from his own face and calls Satan, as if in a direct challenge, not "a true martyr of love." "You are bitter and desolate, for you were dismissed from your early holiness. You did not return from your origin to your end. You left your origin cursed, and in the end, unlike the saints, who did not curse their origins but gave themselves totally to their Beloved in love, you were damned. The spring you drew from is a stagnating pool, sucked dry; you suffer from paucity even where abundance flows; the verdant shade that you covet is only the film that coats your eyes; your leonine fury is only the immobilization of your tamed look; your cutting swords are imaginary; the dark night is a yawning emptiness in which your mannerisms and vanities, ruses and falsehoods, fall away irretrievably into nothing. Ah! there 'it' is!"

He concludes, as if addressing himself: "O brother! If you have understood, you have pondered the narrow pass in its very narrowness; you have shown the imagination in its very unreality, and you have returned from it to reality through sorrow, filled with anxiety.

"The most eloquent of sages keep silent about Satan, lacking the strength to utter what they learn about him:

Satan is more informed than they about worship; he is closer than they to the Being; he has devoted himself more zealously than they to serve Him; he has kept more to his vow than they; he has drawn nearer than they to the Beloved.

"The other angels bowed down before Adam because they were no longer standing, and Satan refused to bow down because he had been in contemplation a long time.

"And yet, alas, he was muddled. He ceased to trust in God. He said "I am worth more than he, Adam!' He remained on this side of the veil, he wallowed in mud and embraced damnation for his eternity of eternities."

The underlying issue to all this is whether humanity has the capacity or incapacity to experience union with God. Massignon's initial assumption, prior to his dramatic experience in the Turkish prison in Iraq, was that man had virtually infinite capacity to discover, but not to unite with, any personal or impersonal God or gods. After that experience he was sure of the existence of "the Absolute," and after his "conversion" to Catholicism, he believed in the accessibility of the personal God and, through those whose relics he carried, in direct union with God. Through his own sacerdotal offering of "sacrifice" he knew intimacy with God. But he did not claim the experience of union for himself, only his recognition of it in a few others. Further, he believed there were two causes among the religiously minded for disbelief in union: personal shyness and fear of presumption, and the predisposition of some minds for philosophical and impersonal detachment. There are different kinds of people and they view transcendence differently, not one good and the other malevolent, however much they may com-

53

pete against each other for worldly power and influence. He clearly mellowed over the years on this point without surrendering his own belief in God's accessibility. Indeed, it formed the cornerstone of his religious life and his stance on other religions and positions. It represented "orthodoxy," and "heterodoxy" was measured against this doctrine.

To him and to al-Hallaj the presence of God was that of Friend and the spirit of love in the world expressed itself spiritually among people as friendship. This, I believe, was the core uniting them: the secret of al-Hallaj's soubriquet "the reader of hearts" and of Massignon's wide-ranging world of "correspondences."

FOREWORD TO PART TWO

From 1959, when I first came to know Louis Massignon, until 1968, when I began to edit and translate his *La Passion d'al-Hallaj*, I kept a diary of accounts of our meetings and, subsequent to his death, of meetings with others who were directly or indirectly associated with him or with the concerns of his life. The diary consists of seven *notebooks* of entries, letters transcribed, and personal reflections on Massignon's thought, on al-Hallaj and his teaching, on Catholicism, on Islam, on personal friendship, on the story of Gilgamesh. They include my various rough sketches and crude preparations for a poetic retelling of the latter story, which I was able to write more simply and fluently when I closed the diary for good. 1968 was also the year Thomas Merton died on his Asian journey and our correspondence, which continued after Massignon's death, came to an abrupt end. I returned to Paris for the first time since Massignon's death in January of that year and traveled beyond to the Near East to acquire Arabic books essential to my translation work. In Ephesus, Turkey, I visited the Cave of the Seven Sleepers, with which account I ended my diary. In 1968 also, my friend the painter Dino Cavallari began to create his own retelling of Gilgamesh, which influenced mine that appeared two years later, in 1970.

The following pages represent an edited selection of

55

entries from the years 1959 and 1960, when I became a regular visitor to Massignon's study at 21 rue Monsieur in the seventh arrondissement. When we met in 1959 I was almost twenty-seven years old, he was seventy-six. I was living abroad in obscurity, writing and translating. He was a retired distinguished professor of the Collège de France and a celebrated activist against the war in Algeria whose name appeared in the newspapers daily and whose acquaintances included those in positions of power. The differences in our backgrounds, ages, and positions in life never seemed an obstacle to our friendship.

The following selections include no accounts of our separate personal lives, families, places of employment, sources of income, and the like, especially in my case inasmuch as I am not the focus of this book. My selection process was guided by respect for the people I knew those years and by my desire to avoid repetition of content and effect in my accounts. My aim was to present an immediate and evocative portrait of Louis Massignon.

PART TWO

Diary, 1959-1960

April 19, 1959—My work of translating Pierre Gabrier's book on St. John of the Cross has me dreaming and waking bolt up in my bed at night. I am not natively a mystic, but I am filled with "considerations." I wonder of the soul as it first discovers the darkness of prayer. I consider introspectively the walls around which voices reverberate, pictures are painted, self-improvised lights turn on: depictions of possible precipices: intensified arguments, partial insights into others' states, judgments of others, hatred of falseness (not yet of one's own), disillusionment with human values, anger at phantoms of beauty or success that vanish leaving one in the bitterness and fatigue of inexperience: hatred which is met and dissolved only by prayer for mercy and patience, by obedience to whatever is given, not imagined, and by humility in the dark places of the soul. The desire for manifestations of freedom, if not calmed within by wisdom, leads the soul pathetically into empty retrievals of lost pasts, into oppressions of others, into disaster for oneself. To such a precipice all the elements and forces lead one to recognize one's irreversible situation, to sensing the fullness of the danger into which one by his own mishandling can plunge himself. Prayer is drawn to but does not love the darkness or the prison in which one waits and hears other's voices, sometimes beautiful and poignant, sometimes delusively heroic, sometimes baleful

59

and sad. What the soul craves from the promised balancing of wisdom with love—conceived in the darkness of prayer—is first the power to embrace the justice of its condition. Such is the necessary stability that still eludes.

I consider writing itself a voluntary fatal engagement, a willful strengthening of the mortal double in one's life. I have been renouncing, even as I have been embracing, it. What is its line of taboo, its threshold of danger, its sacred forest beyond that is mysterious and threatening? The double tries with his fearful life to guard that one thing in us that both makes us human and that we leave invariably unguarded. I begin to sense mortality in my double's trembling as we both, like two friends strengthened by each other to risk danger, run headlong to the threshold. Beyond that doorway the soul rushes, with dangerous presumption and impatience, crying out in fatal joy at the feeling of freedom born of the violation of taboo. The mortal double teaches by his death what it is he guards. What is left when, after a long and solitary journey to wisdom, the truth is finally known? One falls to the ground and weeps in silent sobriety at fate for want of an articulate companion.

I consider the fall of man. As Melville said, it is the most apparent of truths. All else is cloaked in mystery. That fall is revealed to us entirely. Nothing apparently needs to be held back concerning it for our protection. We can make what we want of it; it's ours. Yet alone as a fact it is meaningless. Once fallen as we are, we ourselves are obvious. Satan is disguised in mystery. But Satan also, as fallen angel, is

subject to the obvious, to self-delusion; to the error
of thinking his own thought is luminous, his inspiration divine and not merely his own; to the
disappointment of discovering himself capable of self-
deception; and, finally, to turning that disappointment into rage at God whose light he doesn't love
but envies for its freedom from self-deception. He
tells us then that we have no light, only an abandoned darkness in which he mocks the pathetic beginnings of our tries at prayer. By inventing our
prayer out of nothing, as Satan insists we are doing,
he shows us by his example that we are paralleling
his own invention of disbelief. We are linked in our
inferiorities, and the partnership built on erroneous
sharing of unhappiness is deadly. The soul runs on
in this satanic friendship, the underside of liberating
human friendship based on the acceptance and fruit-
fulness of truth, but satanic creativity craves only
destruction, the liberation from itself. Is the mortification of this erroneous creativity what St. John of the
Cross in his dark humorless way, is trying to teach?
Even to the point of mortifying the prophetic glance
of one's salvation? Is the saint quasi-paranoid, not
without reason, about the soul's capacity for erroneous attachments? Reading and translating him now,
at least in Pierre Gabrier's personalized study of him,
especially after dark, gives me chills. Yet he knows
prayer of which I know nothing. I think he has
dialogued in his prison with God's proud, fallen contemplative Satan, his awesome and frightening
teacher of the negative path of life. Otherwise he
would not know how the law of contradiction is
necessary to salvation.

April 27—I visited Père Jean Daniélou at the Jesuit
house, 15 rue Monsieur; about my third or fourth
conversation with him since we met a year ago
through Madame Abeille, the amiable and people-
collecting friend of Pierre Gabrier, who recently suggested I write Thomas Merton in Kentucky for ideas
regarding eventual dissemination of our St. John of
the Cross enterprise. All these people seem immersed
in their religious paths, so to speak, which include—
and not in a peripheral way—connecting people with
people. This latter "art" may be what makes them
seem anxious, if not superficial. Daniélou particularly
seems always ready to move on, restless in the present; he sizes things up quickly and has no small talk.
It may be uncharitable of me to describe him thus,
but while I am considering the efficacy of prayer and
looking into its friendships, I neither demand nor
pretend that everyone involved in it be saintly or
even moderately wonderful. Being human is enough
to celebrate.

Daniélou is a small, wiry man. He hunches over
the table as he talks. His fingers beat little discordant
tunes on the wooden surface. I don't know him well
enough to ask him to stop. His eyes, hidden partially
behind horn-rimmed glasses, are intense, bright, not
simple in terms of what they see, perhaps not clear.
His mouth twists a little when he speaks. He smiles,
ironically, wittily; he obeys his restlessness, watching
some invisible clock. I've learned that his book pro-
duction has multiplied the further he has strayed
from his actual expertise (the Patristic period of
church history) and he has succumbed at least on
one occasion (that of his celebrated *Lord of History*) to

explain God's work in the world through time. I
looked into the latter work and found it folly. He
spoke on this occasion of Thomas Merton, whom I
have recently written at Gabrier's anxious prodding,
and with whom he exchanges letters regularly, and
who he said "lacks patience." He's "very young," he
said, " and a little too detached." I think he brought
him up to me because of our both being Americans.
Apparently both irony and the obvious abound. He
also mentioned a few more persons he wants me to
meet—partly as my spiritual agent, partly to move
me on beyond himself. One problem for him may be
my own uncertainty as to what I am seeking of him.
The answer is nothing, but I cannot declare nothing
and expect any communication on his part. He is a
customs officer perhaps, one who lets me through on
trust without questioning or becoming involved himself. This time he spoke of Jean-Paul Sartre, Stanislas
Fumet, François Mauriac, and Julien Green, all literary personages, thinking that might be my way. All I
seek really is patience myself, not continuous mobil-
ity or collection. One day I might hold patience in
my hands in wonder and awe, delicately, as one
cups in one's hands and looks through one's fingers
at a firefly.

We spoke of dear Madame Abeille, our mutual ac-
quaintance who holds spiritual salons in her home,
arranges for persons she likes to meet one another in
other people's houses or remote chapels; "a charming
lady," he said, his face lighting up and remaining
still for a moment like my firefly. The charm of
Daniélou is that he doesn't mind being cupped momentarily in another's hands while being utterly in-

capable of containing himself, it seems, even for a second in his own.

May 23—Daniélou wrote a letter of introduction to Mauriac, which I haven't followed up on.

May 31—A gathering at the home of Pierre Gabrier on the occasion of his son's *Communion Solennelle*. Madame Abeille was present and made a point of introducing me to a Dominican priest dressed in a white wool robe—"Oxford education, Egyptian Jew by birth, master of thirty-six languages, a very learned man," she said—named Jean de Menasce, who had recently arrived from the United States, where he had been in residence at the Advanced Institute in Princeton. "He's a friend of the Maritains," she said with awe. His face lighted up at the unexpected appearance of an American at such a private, familial, and French occasion. We spoke of mutual acquaintances at Princeton and Harvard briefly, then of mutual friends in Paris. For some reason, all of a sudden, we began to laugh and couldn't stop. We walked out of the crowded living room and into Pierre's small study and sat down relaxedly, he in Pierre's desk chair and I on his couch, to talk. He asked me if I had encountered Louis Massignon yet, suggesting by his tone and wide-open eyes that this was an original. "I've seen him," I said quietly, knowing that Gabrier and Massignon differed vehemently on the Algerian war and this was Gabrier's home and his son's day. De Menasce understood my prudence, yet I could tell he wanted anxiously to know my impression of Massignon. I wanted to speak at length with this new and *sympathique* person, but another occasion would come one day I knew.

I had a chance on this occasion to speak with Madame Abeille when we found ourselves seated together on a small sofa in one corner of the living room by a window. She said, looking through the thin transparent beige curtain at the boulevard below, "It is all too simple, isn't it?" Her gaze included the guests and the occasion itself.

"What is?" I asked, without meaning to be contentious.

"Can you really believe in God?" she asked me, turning her plumpish, matronly, but quite feminine face as if to study—or "collect"—my response.

"I am trying to understand prayer," I said.

"Ah, but that's quite different," she said, and turned away again. Perhaps I was not to be collected after all, I assumed.

Later, photographs were taken of Pierre, his son, and the other family members, including Pierre's elderly parents, dignified and disapproving-looking Protestants who had arrived by train from their home in Bordeaux. At the end he asked that a photograph be taken of himself with me, his "American translator and friend."

June 3—My Turkish tutee in English, Erten, this morning during this the third of our projected eight sessions preparing her for college entrance examinations in America, called me a materialist and herself a fatalist. She said by "materialist" she meant someone who has lost something of his anonymity to the force

65

of individual will, to putting motion into matter outside himself and therewith and thereby becomes
identified with and by what he has moved. Whereas
she remains anonymous, unidentified with or by anything, part of the unformed immobilized spirit, included in no action in any mass. I was more than a
little unclear as to what she was talking about, but I
told her, briefly, that if this was so, she was freer of
self-deception than I, who might imagine my action
of will has actually accomplished something of consequence. She laughed without the usual irony of
fatalists. She spoke to me again, as she has a little
before, about her Muslim faith. I am curious but not
intrusive.

June 4—Lunch at the elegant rue Corneille apartment of Arnold Smit, the South African diplomat
who went through the process of converting to Catholicism (in his case, from Calvinism) and whom I
met during my own seemingly less drastic process
over a year ago. He is six feet four or five inches and
grotesquely bony with extremely long fingers and
long crossed legs, two unmistakable signs of the very
rich, which he is. He invited me and the secretary to
Cardinal Marella (the Papal Nunzio in Paris who con-
firmed us together), a Mgr Binelli from Florence. Arnold's usual sidekick from his embassy, Jeremy, and
Jeremy's friend from Oxford days, Peter, a painter,
were not included on this occasion. Just the three of
us, served by Arnold's live-in Spanish maid. Arnold
is reading the classical Jesuits and doing the Spiritual
Exercises of St. Ignatius. He's very enthusiastic. After
lunch he played for us on his grand piano, which
stands against the even grander background of an

only slightly faded eighteenth-century floral and hunting tapestry, a composition in honor of his conversion. He said it was inspired in part by a prayer of Claudel's from the play *Le Soulier de satin* and was written as a variation on two themes: the bells at Burgos and a Gregorian chant from the Angelus. It was brief, lyrical, enchantingly danced, as it were, by his faerylike fingers across the keys. Afterwards we had a conversation about art and the Devil. It was like a scene from Huysman's *A rebours* or perhaps *En route*. Perhaps it will float back to me sometime. At present I've forgotten what we said. I remember only Mgr Binelli clapping his little hands in glee.

June 5—Received this morning an ebullient letter from Yvonne Chauffin. She mentioned me to Professor Massignon. His address is 21 rue Monsieur; his phone SUF 36-69. Daniélou's street. This week my correspondents, les Mesdames Chauffin et Abeille et le Père Daniélou, have thus far arranged for me to meet in violent succession Mauriac, Massignon, a Benedictine Dom Masabke, and Gabriel Marcel, to what end I'm not sure. If someone asked me what I want in such interviews, I would have no answer. Meetings of this kind may be reassuring to some, useless to others.

Yvonne is sending me from her Breton home *Berluhec* her new novel *La Brûlure* via her publisher in Paris. She hopes I can attend the Muslim-Christian pilgrimage in Brittany in July. She invites me to her house near Quimperlé on that occasion. We met originally through Pierre Gabrier, to whom she tells me she can't write anymore because of his extremist views on Algeria. And he can no longer write to her because of her extremist views on Algeria. She wrote that Massignon once told her, "Laissez les mondanités littéraires. Nous sommes faits pour ressusciter les morts."

If I were to burn bridges the way my French friends do, I would have no friends. Somehow they both *do* and *do not* believe in their renunciations.

June 10—A letter came from Thomas Merton this morning. I forget what I wrote in my last letter to him, following my inquiries about St. John of the Cross, that is. From his I gather that I wrote of his booklet on Prometheus, his poem *Landfall*, and on spiritual journey in general. His was dated June 6 and sent from his abbey, Our Lady of Gethsemani, Trappist, Kentucky.

Dear Herbert:

Your paragraph on Prometheus echoes very exactly and sums up what I have been driving at. I am glad P. Daniélou gave you the booklet. It is true that there is a certain nobility in fighting for what we already have, because if we fail to do this we do not really have it. But it is best to remember that we already have it and that everything does not depend on the fighting. It is the great mystery of grace. Not grace in the sense of a kind of theological gasoline that you get by performing virtuous actions (that is the sin we commit!) but grace in the fact that God has given Himself completely to us already. Completely. But we have to enter into the darkness of His presence. Not tragic darkness, just ordinariness: but above all what does not appear to be religion.

I tell you frankly that my present struggle with the institutional aspect of religion is enormous and almost overwhelming. It is tempting to ruin the whole thing by dramatizing it as something Promethean, as if truth were something I had to conquer and bring back into the ruins. They are cold and without fire, really. The fire that is there has nothing to do with the external forms which people so carefully preserve. (Perhaps here I exaggerate, through excessive reaction.) The only issue is in a paradox of great humility, a small door through which one goes out, appearing to be nothing: and having become nothing—that is the liberation.

The journey goes with this. No, I have not read Melville for years and years. And the *Landfall* goes back ten years. The journey is present every day. Better, the voyage. The nothing which happens every day has to be an adventure, and it is. To be Prometheus and to be on a voyage is almost the same thing. It is out of the nothing, the void, of our own self that we freely create the paradise in which we walk with God. This act of creation is—grace. It is all a gift. Grace out of nothingness. The image of a landfall is one of the obvious ones for this daily awakening. I especially like P. Daniélou's chapter on *epectasis* in the book on Gregory of Nyssa (still his best).

I am glad you know P. Daniélou. Give him my regards, please, and remind him that he owes me a letter.

> With very best wishes—
> God bless you,
> Fr. Louis

June 8—I met Professor Massignon this morning in his study at 21 rue Monsieur for two hours. He is a specialist on the Near East and in particular on the Muslim faith. He knows Gilgamesh's story well, which he said is also enclosed in the Qur'an. I did not know this. He referred to *sura* 18, "The Cave." I have been aware dimly of the Qur'an's enclosure of Christ and the Judaic law and prophetic tradition. But Massignon's and my conversation about Gilgamesh and, later, his introduction of a Muslim mystic named al-Hallaj deepened immeasurably my sense of the epic as the dramatic structure of spiritual experience. I felt relief in his presence, the relief that comes from someone older who knows who one is and asks no questions for accreditation.

He told me of his life in the Near East, his living as a Muslim (I supposed in disguise)—in Iraq, I believe; his imprisonment as a suspected French spy—by the Turks, I believe; his three days of spiritual trial ("épreuve"). He was chained and interrogated. He believed these physicial chains, however, were nothing in comparison to the chains of his own sins. For the first time in his life he realized he was being judged, not by man alone, but by God. It was in 1907 or 08, I think he said; he spoke fast in a flood of words and images. My attentive, no, enrapt ear was a little rowboat at best against the overwhelming waves. I think he was twenty-four or twenty-five years old at the time of his imprisonment, more or less my own age (now twenty-seven). His interrogators twisted truths into useless lies trying to get confession from him, and he realized for the first time that there was such a thing as truth. He used the expression *the snows and ice of sin*; he spoke of walking across those, of being lost on a frozen lake without any markers; and he called out, believing that if there was a rock anywhere, the echo would come back; and it came back. He realized in himself the totality of impurity—and the presence of purity— and he tried to commit suicide to clear the air of himself for the sake of this purity. Christians do not believe in suicide, yet he said this was his offering to God; this was his entrance to the Land of Vision. In abject poverty and filth he was God's witness. He was the discoverer at that moment, for those three days, of the fact that we are "condemned" to immortality. We discover that all our desires go out to dying things, to multiplications of ideas that are doomed already. That God's allness is, in fact, an endless multiplicity of ideas we will never discover through any of our desires. That we are, however, set in existence, to live with this existence and, as Christians, to be bound by love to Christ and to use our bond to free others. At the core of God is liberty, he said, and His gift of love to man is this liberty. It is our calling to return this love to God. He says the Indian Hindu believes too much that existence is an illusion—it is not. He said he has no solution to make the world all right. He knows rather that man must suffer, that man must atone. That heaven and hell are creations and that the human person lives somewhere between—between—when all is God.

He said he is a tertiary Franciscan and told me of the shame of many Franciscans in Paris for building with American money a palace when many people could be "freed" with that money.

71

He (meaning humanity, Christ, all of us?) lives with the poor; he lives in humiliation—by his friends, by his relatives—and he knows what the poor know, the emptiness and impurity. He knows God. Forty-two years a Catholic and two hours every morning, he said,he is with God. (I did not understand these references, which he chose not to explain.) When one knows God in humiliation and poverty one wants no crown, one needs no crown.

He told me of the "dishonesty" of Cardinal Spellman and Tammany Hall in New York, yet, he said, "I'm sure he prays." His smile was sardonic and bitter.

He told me, above all, of his intellectual apprehension during those three days (in Iraq?), of the persons who were praying for him: his mother, Sister Violet Sussman, Léon Bloy, Huysmans, Père Charles de Foucauld, and al-Hallaj who had been dead for 1000 years, and another person whose name I forget. (I'm not sure now if all of these prayed *then* or at *other times*, there were so many names and overlappings of times). He apprehended them in their prayers for him. And when he was freed and returned to Paris he met his mother, who had been at Lourdes, and Huysmans, who was suffering with cancer of the throat, yet who had prayed for him upon his mother's request, and others as well.

When I stepped back, internally so to speak, from these accounts, I found myself tossed about between fascination and skepticism; but in the midst of the flood itself I could only hold to the sides of my inexperienced skiff. I had never met any narrator like Massignon, who was instantly wild and exaggerative, sharp and believable. Part of his credibility was in his eyes, his face, his hands, his book-lined study surrounding him, the books themselves, especially those that dealt with remote subjects and places written in (to me) unreadable languages. His eyes were deep-socketted, wide open, clear, yet often burning with intense fire, then suddenly cooling, calm, compassionate, kindly, uninvasive. His cheeks were sunken in, lined with little cross walks, weathered deeply, toughened like parchment. His little hair was white, tussled. His hands were moving constantly, illustrating, orchestrating memories that were still live events to him. He as a living person seemed apart from time yet showed its pains and ravages in his eyes and face and the wild rhythms of his hands. He had been, I knew, where I had never gone. I didn't doubt for a moment that he was the person I had come to meet.

At a pause in this our first meeting he asked me to pray for him and I asked him to pray for me.

He told me of his trip last year to Japan. He went to pay his debt of love to Violet Sussman. He saw in the poverty of Tokin (?) the living seed of her work. He visited her grave, fixing a paper cross on it.

One instant only, he said, one instant is enough to spend the rest of one's life in love, wanting nothing else.

He told me of an army colonel who came to his home recently, a believer in "the modern illness, technocracy," wanting to tear God out of these Muslims' hearts by machinery. The colonel ended his visit in tears. "He may hold it against me because I made him wet." He said this with a look of sadness,

73

not delight. I think I know very little about compassion.

He spoke of his sin of pride, its paralyzing moments in his life. He closed his eyes, struggling for a passage of a text he wanted me to know. Then he seemed to yield and said "In the Annunciation the Virgin is most conscious of her unworthiness. It is incautious of us to think only of her Assumption, her crown." I noticed tears in his eyes.

He spoke of his meeting and correspondence with Gandhi and some yogis of India, of their basic desire to be free. They fear the Occident enslaves, he said. "Yet men and women are occasioned by God's love; this freedom is neither East nor West."

He told me he has had to ask God twice: "Enough! Enough!" He said he is not able to suffer actively too much. More and more he is becoming pacific, like Gandhi, who he said sometimes however "played tricks."

He gave me a Huysmans biography by an Englishman to read and an article of his own published 20 Mai in *Les Lettres nouvelles*: "La Guerre Sainte suprême de l'Islam."

He shared with me a *qissa Husayn al-Hallaj* in which a mystic threw a rose at the gibbet of the dying saint. In his rendering: "cette pauvre herbe n'est qu'un jeu pour moi, je ne puis me contenter qu'en le contemplant."

Hours later I was interrupted frequently in my reading by the recollection of Massignon's face, his sudden bursts of joy, his gaze of pity and remorse. The contrasts, especially his joy, makes him seem a little mad, a little inebriated, like that madness of which St. Paul in his best moments speaks.

The *qissa* remained with me through the night and I knew that I had not only met Massignon but also al-Hallaj:

"Je ne cessais de nager sur les mers de l'amour, montant avec le vague, et puis redescendant . . . . "

"Husayn, when they threw stones at you, you laughed; when one throws a rose, you weep. He answers: don't you know how hard it is for the lover to feel the injustice of his beloved?"

I woke up in the night alarmed by Massignon's word "atone."

June 9—I met Mauriac at his home today—for approximately five minutes, all he could spare. He asked me to return next Wednesday, I'm not sure why. He spoke quickly and briefly about "the Catholic literary tradition" of France, one among several mutually respecting and respected French traditions, which I assume he thought I was inquiring about. He spoke obliquely about the general outlook of American Catholics, about which I know virtually nothing. Odd, his presuppositions. He was cordial, correct. It was this visit that unearthed the word *tradition*. I felt on trial as a foreigner. He sat in a large armchair in his receiving room beside a sculptured bust of himself atop a handsome teak stand. I sat on the visitors couch. It was clear, I'm sure, to us both that neither of us had any interest in or curiosity about the other. He made a reference of Camus, for public consumption through me, I guessed: "He is not a very important writer. Sartre's much more important." I'm afraid such Literary business fell on deaf ears.

All afternoon, following this rather awkward visit, I was haunted by the memory of Massignon, by his strong, distinct character, and by his joy. I knew that a year before, or even a few weeks before, I would have been much more impressed and absorbed by Mauriac or other notable writers. Perhaps not. In any case, Massignon has changed all that. I wrote a note to Yvonne Chauffin thanking her for her introduction. I may have mentioned Massignon to Mauriac, I don't recall now; if so, it may be for this reason that he invited me back. I think they have some political affinities on Algeria; or it's something else.

June 10—Madame Abeille phoned to say she would accompany me to Gabriel Marcel's apartment on rue de Tournon, a stone's throw from Arnold Smit's near the Théâtre Odéon, Place de Claudel. Pierre Gabrier calls her a connoiseur of great men. He says I should be flattered, especially as a foreigner, to be so favored by her. (And to think, all this just because I walked into a bookstore on rue de Vieux Colombier and happen to be struck by the painting of St. John of the Cross on the cover of one Pierre Gabrier's book.) He said she delights in such men's "victoires d'ésprit et d'intellect." Recently she featured a famous Protestant theologian at one of her salons. He spoke of his dramatic conversion from atheistic materialism. When I spoke to her of meeting Massignon, she told me of the celebrated demonstration in the Palais Royale against the war led by Mauriac, Sartre, and Massignon walking arm in arm.

The mob was angry, she said, over the deplorable conditions in Algeria. Only Massignon of the three, she said with light irony, has ever seen them firsthand. He's the only one whose "fierceness," as she put it, is deeply rooted. "Did you like him?" she asked.

Pierre Gabrier phoned me soon after. He was upset when I mentioned Massignon. I felt from his reaction that he considered I had betrayed our friendship by meeting this "radical." Algeria is (between them, it appears) one of those cataclysmic affairs that divides a nation regardless of common belief and tradition. It allows no compromise, apparently. Gabrier and Massignon, unbeknown to me, have not spoken to one another since the Palais Royale incident. Gabrier, also unknown to me until this morning, had been Minister of Algerian Affairs at the time, and rang up Massignon the next day and demanded: "Qu'est-ce que tu fait?" They fought. Massignon accused Gabrier of closing his eyes to the truth of political imprisonments without cause, of torture of prisoners, of immoral actions not acceptable to France. Gabrier accused Massignon of inciting to riot by his so-called "moral demonstration" by, in Gabrier's word, "immoralists." He said he can accept Mauriac because he's at least behind deGaulle, whom Gabrier served with in the Resistance and who he hopes will be strong toward "the enemy"; but he can't forgive the "unruliness" of a man of Massignon's knowledge and stature, of his willful association with disorder in the streets. He dismissed Sartre out-of-hand as "a failed member of the bourgeoisie, an atheist" whose "sarcasm is as well

77

known as the ugliness of his face." When Gabrier hung up I sat shivering, wondering what I had stumbled into. Gabrier's wrath sounded more like jealousy than politics. But of whom?

June 12—Madame Abeille phoned and said G. Marcel is due back in Paris soon. She told me she had seen Père Jean de Menasce again and he told her L. Massignon is the "génie du siècle."

June 13—Gabrier phoned. This time I let slip that Madame Abeille was taking me soon to meet Marcel. He said Marcel "is a fool. He believes in seances and palm readers, and so does Madame Abeille!" *Pierre Gabrier*, the pseudonym by which my original introducer prefers to be known, writes articles for Catholic papers, gives speeches on behalf of "Algérie française" groups, holds now a rather lowly functionary job in the government, and is nearly exhausted in his eyes and voice by the burden of his fanaticism.

June 17—The second visit with Mauriac today was longer than last week's. Again, he instructed me in "tradition." "In letters," he said, "I'm afraid I'm the last [*le dernier*]. The Lord has no need of men of letters now, only saints." He attacked the American church for being only political. He described deGaulle as a man with a dynamic gift of remaining open to possibilities with his storehouse of ideas. (I thought of Massignon's words about God's infinity of ideas and man's limitations for realizing them—in contrast.) He described reunification of Germany as dangerous. (I suspected this purely literary man had lost a sense of his limitations on a number of fronts. He referred to a few noted Catholic figures as "imbeciles." He omitted mention of Massignon altogether.) He asked me if I had met Dom Masabke at the rue de la Source abbey, in his own Passy district, yet. I said no but that it was to be arranged. He said "good. I'm very close to him. He's my confessor." He paused and gazed in silence for a few seconds, then added: "He's a saint."

June 19—21 rue de Tournon, Gabriel Marcel's apartment. Madame Abeille met me downstairs in the hallway. I truly had no interest in any further meetings with "great men" but could not escape this prearranged rendezvous. It was a kind of salon in Marcel's very sparsely furnished and drab living room. Several people surrounded "le maître" while he spoke, all attentive to his pauses and silences. I have little patience for such occasions, I realize. Marcel himself was friendly. He let himself be waited on by everyone. Someone volunteered to drive him across town for a later rendezvous. He seems very soft, a pudgy aesthete of sorts with soft gray bangs over his forehead and a fluffy gray moustache that is too long and makes him sneeze every so often. Quite a contrast to the aquiline face, the lean and arched body, and mean inclining look of his co-religionist Mauriac. Marcel, though noted as a Catholic existentialist philosopher, spoke mostly of the theatre on this occasion and was droll about his own unsuccessful attempts to write for it. He said without any apparent bitterness or envy that he hated Claudel's *L'Otage*

79

("an affront to human nature as it is") and told with remarkable modesty and reverence of being instrumental in persuading an editor to publish Bernanos' *Diary of a Country Priest* ("one of France's great novels"). All the while he was commenting and reminiscing I was feeling reconfirmed in my sense of being at the end of the Catholic literary renascence, and it did not feel especially fruitful to witness ends.

He had been to Michigan recently, he said, to attend a World Conference on Moral Rearmament (which Mauriac had included among things "imbecilic"). He said he enjoyed his visit to America and Americans in general. In contrast to his Catholic colleagues he seemed lacking in judgmentalism, perhaps also in judgment. He moved more leisurely than some from subject to subject, being perhaps more cognizant of his audience's varied intelligences and nationalities. One Swiss student told me aside that Marcel is very generous with his time. "He helps a lot of us in philosophy at the Sorbonne, though he is not appointed there." How does he live? I wondered. Another said "through patronage." Marcel praised Julien Green generously, closed his eyes prudently when a student injected the name "Massignon" into a brief discussion of "contemporary politics," and chased his enormous white angora cat across the living room and scolded it after it bit my hand.

Madame Abeille took particular care of a rather shy Moroccan student and wrote down her phone number for him to call in case of need or if, as she put it, he just wanted a good meal or conversation.

Marcel summed up by noting the evening's absence of philosophical questions of him, but praised sociability and hoped his American guest would forgive his cat.

June 20—Gabrier phoned and railed coincidentally at Marcel for not attacking communism more vigorously in print. He said the world is overtaken already by evil forces and France stands alone as the last hope against them all. His is another—the unhealthy—kind of madness. I think he does not know how to deal with ends. But do I know enough to say that?

June 21—This morning with Professor Massignon again in his study. I tried at first to detach a little in order to understand him or at least to place him in the proverbial scheme of things: as a *provocateur*, an *avocat du diable*, a cracker of shells that encrust themselves on human souls, most surprisingly his own before he assaults others'. His particular *bête-noir*, like Dante's, seems to be professional church-men, Christians who behave possessively of Christ—that is, uncharitably toward others and thereby con-tradicting Christ's offering of himself selflessly to others. I hear him automatically and spontaneously defining Christianity in terms of compassion, not the-ological speculation. One of his verbal salvos whizzed thus: "Maritain is the only theologian whose writing doesn't make me sick to read." I hadn't indicated that even Maritain's theology itself turned me off. The salvo was quite gratuitous. Apparently they are very old friends. They met, he said, many years ago at the front door of Massignon's present home when they both coincidentally were following separate leads of

81

an apartment for rent. I suspect Maritain is one of
the few whom Massignon will not criticize on some
level. Whereas Claudel as a friend was not immune,
on this occasion, from such epithets as "pompous
ass."

I composed myself by recognizing that friendship
among Christians, as among any other group, is not
to be confused with niceness or even civility.
Massignon this morning bit into a few prominent
church officials savagely. He devoured their abuses of
innocence, betrayals of trust, arrogance of position,
manipulations of power at the expense of the power-
less. It's a bit tough on the outsider or the newcomer
who wants to believe in the purity of the church and
faces the visible church before entering the invisible
church. Indeed, his rage seems almost satanic, or at
the very least Voltairian, in the disguise of a believer,
as if Massignon among all the French Catholic circle
of friends was the one in whom the Pascalian and
Voltairian *traditions* were actually combined. The
result of this paradoxical fusion on this occasion was
a guided brief descent past the vestibule of commonplace faults into a few bolgias of our contemporary inferno. As a guide he threw light like a holy
man on the devilish, though both the Devil's and the
saint's faces were merged as masks covering his own.
Indeed, what his strange holiness begins to reveal to
me, intentionally or unintentionally, is that Satan's
face by contrast with the saint's is devoid of
passion—is detached, cold, ironic, recoiling smugly at
any suggestion of passionate concern or care to
which, on the other extreme, the conventional saint
too readily and simply succumbs. To the holy lover

of God, I begin to believe, God is passion itself; his
rage is his Beloved's rage; his care is Love's care;
there is nothing detached or clever about it; passion
exceeds both the coolly rejecting angel's and the
humbly accepting saint's comprehension, defying the
one's ironic detachment and the other's sentimentality. Massignon is explosive. He is consistent without
being predictable. I had no idea before meeting him
that holiness was something other than clever intellect or pious civility. In him it is struggle—
wrestling—as if to the death with each. But more, it
is passionate Love of the Beloved neither truly knows
and whom each would have us believe by their
mockingly dispirited attitudes is inaccessible to us
humans. At that Massignon explodes—in his heart, in
his flesh.

I begin to pick up through others and readings
here and there certain facts about his Life; but while
such facts seem significant, I'm not sure of their
relevance to what moves him. He was apparently a
frontline lieutenant and an intelligence officer during
and following the First World War. He knew Lawrence of Arabia. Both were involved in some way in
the execution of the Sykes-Picot plan for the control
of Palestine. Massignon referred today two or three
times to himself as "an outlaw," a Melkite, not a
Latin Catholic; a Muslim among Muslims. Madame
Abeille told me of his voluntary teaching of math and
basic French to North African immigrant laborers.
And, of course, he's retired as a professor of the Collège de France. He earned his money from his professional academic position, but she also informed me
that he came from an upper middle-class Parisian

83

family that left him some inheritance, most of which he "has given foolishly away to needy relatives, friends, and strangers." He travels so frequently and freely, she said, because he enjoys diplomatic status dating from his days as cultural ambassador of France to the Near East after 1918. All of which is fascinating but reveals nothing of his spirit and its explosiveness.

We talked about the Gilgamesh story again and about pilgrimage: what it means to leave the place where one belongs for a place hidden beyond where the rivers meet. What it means to seek freedom from one's mortality, this terrible thing we can't escape and which we try to externalize and transfer to others and to nature, both of which we objectify as evil because of their unwillingness to assume for us what is our fate. We strike down the forest of Humbaba, but we do not escape. Only with the death of a friend, Enkidu, do we begin to bear with loss and desire to live more fully, more humanely, not merely for the moment for ourselves. Pilgrimage reveals the soul's "immortal longings" and transforms living into quest for eternal life.

The journey is long. The darkness is deep. There are miles and miles of trees and hills. There is a welcomer at a house, a face of the dying memory, and others the mad mind sees as scorpions, a man and a woman guarding the path beyond themselves and bickering, while the soul lowers the eyes and passes under their gaze, which is death. The dark water is filled with the current of gliding snakes. The boat eases out from the shore. The oars dissolve and the boat drifts across the water with the dark currents at night. One hears a voice on the other shore. One rests and then wakes to the other's explanation of the flood—the other's outcry for justice.

The journeyer has been warned by dreams but now craves only freedom, hinted of in the other's words, and seeks only ecstasy. He runs to the water where the sacred plant was found, dives down, and seizes it. He rises in ecstasy, holding his desired life. And carrying it home for himself or his friend or both—no matter which or whom, since it is of himself he is thinking—he leaves it unguarded by a pool in which he bathes. A serpent comes and devours the plant, leaving it behind as slough.

When he arises from the pool he sees the slough and he sits on the bank and weeps: in emptiness, in nothing; that is the liberation.

Massignon shared with me the memory of his eldest son Yves's death. "When I became a tertiary," he said in English suddenly, "I took the name Abraham. But God did not give me back my son, who died in my arms."

He also shared with me the memory of a close Spanish friend's suicide. He said he based his faith on the hope of his friend's salvation. He said he adopted his friend's father as his own, his friend's father who had suffered so much over his son's suicide. He said he offered his own skeptic father to God for this other's salvation. Two days later his father died in perfect health while at work on a statue of his only Christian friend, Huysmans. To him and, he said, to Maritain, this revealed the salvation of these cherished disbelieving and despairing souls.

I can't say this left me in a state of complete credulity but it mesmerized me as a narrative, as had our sharing of Gilgamesh together.

Once, he continued, seemingly inexhaustible, he had wanted to join Charles de Foucauld in his hermitage in the desert (he said Foucauld believed you could will the soul toward love, "but what has the soul to give?" he paused as if asking me, then answered: "Nothing"). He jerked suddenly to a halt and said angrily that his own biography meant nothing to him, at least nothing he wanted to order for anyone's consumption. I sensed that what he may have been doing by this scattering of bits of it here and there through his flood of words was to throw it away like his inheritance, seeing in it no utility for himself and little of interest to others. None of it seemed graspable or noteworthy to him, I could see by the surrender in his face. I expected any moment a lament, but then, without any warning, I saw a strange smile of joy and I couldn't control my own eyes which had become unpredictably moist. We began simultaneously to laugh and cry. Could anyone fathom this man? Could Maritain?

He spoke in calm of the hardship his wife and surviving son and daughter endured living with his "madness," "with one who loves God Who is invisible more even than those visible who need my help." He spoke of the pleasure of his wife now that he is old and has to spend more time at home. He spoke of the prayers—the deep prayers—he offered during a voyage to Moscow years before when the Russian secret police sent a prostitute into his train compartment, to the upper bunk, and of "the pricking brace-

86

let" he had on his arm that a nun had given him—a
Franciscan bracelet—that got him out of that compartment and led to his actually becoming a tertiary. He
had French government permission to visit Moscow
as an official, though he was going there as a
scholar. And the secret police knew the only way
they could hold him up was on a disorderly conduct
charge. The way the story unfolded accompanied by
a wild array of facial and finger illustrations was ter-
ribly funny and had me weeping with laughter.

One person he and the others I have met in France
mention off and on is the *Ministre de Justice* Michelet
(most names seem to begin with *M*; just kidding),
who was a great Resistance fighter, who also spoke
at the Charles de Foucauld night at the Sorbonne
when I first saw Massignon's face, as it were, on
stage, before I imagined meeting him could be possible. Marcel refers to him as "the most Christian man
he has known." Massignon, when I entered his
study this morning, was shouting at him over the
telephone to "put an end to this infernal practise of
detaining political suspects without cause and to the
torture which follows!" Massignon seems unim-
pressed by reputations, which makes me glad in his
presence that I have none and no reason for calling
on him other than to know him.

He seemed very tired on this occasion, though this
didn't deter him from speaking on. At one point he
said, "DeGaulle is a very proud but an honest man;
unfortunately the circumstances surrounding him are
so very grave." He decried the misuse by so many of
the name of St. Joan, whom he holds dear but also
"unworthily," he said. He said he is very sick at

87

heart over the "rottenness" in both the church and state. "Our ideologies and technologies will condemn man to a pathetic idealism of a terrestrial dying paradise, perhaps only because of the failure of Christians to release their charity."

"Have you clothed the naked, fed the hungry, nursed the sick, visited prisoners . . . ? These are the words," he said, "Christ has a right to ask us now and at the Final Judgment."

He spoke of addressing a group of government officials and military men among whom he had status on the issue of conscientious objectors, of opponents to war and to particular wars. He said to them, "They are not cowards." He repeated loudly in my presence, "They are not cowards!"

He told of an Arab boy who stayed with him once at a certain desert ruin (in Morocco? in Iraq?) when hostile Arab soldiers came, forty in all, he said, surrounding his party of seven, most of whom, save for himself and the boy, ran away. He looked around and saw that this boy had waited.

He said he believes friendship, like this boy's who was willing to die, is the cornerstone of human spiritual life, not family.

One surprise to me, in retrospect, is to realize that these accounts, bearable on the lips only of someone like him, are devoid of cliché. His secret thus far eludes me. At a conference held recently by the military chiefs of staff, including deGaulle, he was invited, as the newspapers reported, to tell what he thought could be the solution of the country's grave problems (especially with regard to Muslim Algeria). He said quite matter-of-factly that if the conference ignores God in its very essence, meaning, and reason for being and as to its total hope, then the results will be meaningless; and hopes in the heart, not merely on the lips! If we cannot share another's sufferings and hopes, then we cannot share; we are then hypocrites.

He talked now of standing between two men who were fighting—neither is right exclusively. War is not right exclusively, but some things are known only in war. You must stand between them, because it will be evident to both that to hit a third is absurd.

Slap the cheek that is right and the cheek that is wrong for both create crime.

He spoke finally in a quiet voice, with tears filling his eyes, of the sexually tortured Algerian girl whom he and Sartre had managed to free from her French captors and hide secretly outside Paris. "I do not understand the pleasure some men get from torturing."

June 24—This morning I woke early and through my window watched men cleaning the street below while pigeons weaved overhead. The strange and terrible mundaneness of this task, this push at dawn along the gutters toward a little flowing clarity, awed me.

Coming back to me, juxtaposed, was one of Massignon's statements: "To understand the other, one does not need to annex him but to become his guest."

Later I went to Gabrier's apartment in Neuilly to go over some aspects of my translation of his book. His ten-year-old daughter, Patrice, ran into his study

89

where we were working and threw her arms around his neck. His whole face lit up. She ran out and afterwards he sat for a minute or two in silence, very calm and happy seeming.

After awhile, alas, he succumbed to his obsession with the Palais Royale: Massignon, Mauriac, and Sartre. Underneath it all I think he is trying to utter his own cry.

Late in the day I met Arnold Smit in a café on Ile de St. Louis, a favorite one just at the Pont Louis Philippe. He was with Jeremy and Peter and someone I didn't know, whom Arnold introduced as John, a newcomer from South Africa. John was explaining his idea about Europeanizing Africa under a strict Christian segregation in order to oppose the dangers of communism and black nationalism. The argument was so stale as to be silly and I thought at first he was playing a lame and idle devil's advocate. Arnold, despite Jeremy's and Peter's not too subtle glances of embarrassment, took him quite seriously and said in his gravest Undersecretary tone, "How can you use the word *Christian* in connection with segregation?" The man's silent sneer suggested he was more mad than silly. Evidently he was an unexpected "embassy guest" and they were showing him a little corner of Paris. After the present round of drinks were finished Arnold rose like a gaunt specter in diplomatic livery and suggested he and John stroll to Notre Dame for a brief tour. He managed to look correct while exuding distaste. They departed and we three remained for another round. Jeremy, a more graceful and intelligent devil's advocate, baited me and Arnold (*in absentia*) gently for our religious enthusiasm, adding by way of a compliment that I seemed the more relaxed of the two of us. I said it was my familial tradition of deceptive calm and he shouldn't be fooled by it. He smiled and said it was a good response. "I think Arnold's about to bolt," he said. "From what?" I asked. "His career. He no longer cares what he says to spies." Our eyebrows lifted simultaneously, then we sat in silence drinking and gazing at the bridge in the late afternoon light. Peter said he wanted us all to come to a party at his flat on rue Jacob in about three weeks. He was doing some new and for him quite different still-life painting and wanted us to see the results. His mother was coming from England. I said I would like to come. After awhile we left the café, Jeremy for his flat in the Marais off place des Vosges, Peter and I toward our respective burrows on the Rive Gauche. Peter, more than Jeremy or Arnold, though all are tall, thin, and handsome, has the air of the classic boy hero, the knightly journeyer, the *puer aeternus* about him: the long pensive look, the graceful stride, the ease of manner; yet he seems also wounded in some indefinable way or perhaps, despite his air of natural charm and talent, believes too little in himself. He's self-enclosed, so our walk through the web of narrow streets to his own of rue Jacob, where we diverged, was quiet.

A few streets away I saw in the window of a curio shop a good copy of a Chinese statue in the Louvre of a father and a son laughing together into the funny look each sees in the other's face.

At home again, I closed my door, looked at the walls, and realized what the day was really all about

91

for me. I need to draw back. Massignon reads my heart, and St. John of the Cross's word *annihilation* is too much for me to bear just now. The poet may be a tertiary in his heart but religion may destroy his nature. The aesthetics of it, not the spirit, is oppressive. I have not yet found my own release in nakedness. I cannot be clothed in others' dress. I crave a few days, alone and anonymous, just walking in my *quartier* or anywhere.

June 25—This morning a *pneumatique* letter was pushed under my door by the concièrge. It was from Gabrier. It included a kind of veiled apology for his talking politics so much and expressed his pleasure at the meetings we have. He said friendship with its laughter of the heart is, quoting Bernanos, "comme le prelude à la musique du ciel" (like the prelude to the music of Heaven).

June 29—After four days and nights of complete seclusion I was ferreted out and taken to lunch by Yvonne Chauffin, in from Brittany for a few days of publisher's parties and book signings. She spoke of *La Brûlure* and of the actual burning of her dead child's clothes and possessions twenty years after the child's death. She said grief had become, as her husband perceived, "a duty." We must release our deepest attachments, she said, because of their intrusion on others. She told me for my better understanding of Pierre Gabrier that he had lost his eldest son, his first-born, in a drowning accident on Lake Geneva. He was France's emissary there after the war and his family was together again and happy for the first time since the war had forced their separation. He cannot release his son's things, she said simply. He is still filled with grief.

July 3—I attended a mass and a Muslim recitation of the Qur'an, both in a church off boulevard Monparnasse, and afterwards a meeting in an adjacent hall attended by Madame Abeille, Yvonne, a few Algerians, others, at which Professor Massignon spoke. Only about fifteen or twenty people were present. He spoke at the end of visiting the Shinto shrine of Isé in Kyoto, "an old lonely mind, overflowed with shyness."

At the time, before he began to speak, I wondered why so few were there for such an important person. Is this the neglect that comes with age? We are interested in a demonstration, but perhaps we run off a distance when threatened with too much knowledge or intimacy.

There is an Arab saying I heard somewhere: "Oh let him die; then we shall know how to aid him."

It was a painful occasion for me, for one does not meet such a man and not love deeply.

When we entered the church for the mass he took blessed water on his fingers and then touched mine with his.

From time to time I have wondered why I am present at these occasions, invited into these friendships, feeling like an eavesdropper, someone not sharing their memories of the German Occupation, the debacle in Indochina, the Algerian war, the personal losses, or their age and longevity. I am not a student in any formal sense, yet I am witnessing their sufferings and their wisdoms surely not as a passing observer.

One of the Muslims present invited me afterwards to visit his mosque and to share dinner with him and his friends. Massignon overheard the invitation and told me it was a good thing. These people, he said, are despised here and so few will sit with them—at a loss to themselves—for they have such a rich spiritual treasury. I accepted.

July 10—This morning I set forth from memory a bare outline with commentary for myself of a retelling of the Gilgamesh story.

i

1. Gilgamesh—the soul, experienced in a worldly sense but suffering from the fatigue of inexperience in the spiritual sense.

The people want to arouse him from his state of self-indulgence, lethargy, and insensitivity in the city of Uruk he is allowing to fall into ruin, he their king.

2. Creation of Enkidu—the animal-man, discovered by hunters among the animals at the watering place—he delights in their companionship.

3. Hunter, whose traps Enkidu opens, thus freeing his brothers the animals, reports to his father, who fears the loss of their livelihood, their way of life. The son is sent to Gilgamesh in Uruk, who tells him, as the father suggested, to send a harlot (a courtesan) to Enkidu who will separate him from the wild animals of the steppe.

4. The seduction of Enkidu by the harlot. The wild animals are estranged and withdraw from him as predicted, leaving him afraid. The harlot tries to build up his courage, to make him a man, to exercise the power he has. She portrays Gilgamesh as an unjust ruler, a rival.

5. In Uruk, Gilgamesh lives in the temple, the inner sacred enclosure, unaware as yet of the rivalry.

6. Enkidu becomes the protector of the hunters, killing the lion. He presumes to conquer his rival Gilgamesh. The harlot now pretends to warn the innocent-seduced one.

7. Gilgamesh dreams—the fallen star. His mother, Ninsun, explains the coming of the stranger. A second dream heightens the apprehension.

ii

1. Gilgamesh dreams of a vying.

2. Enkidu blocks his passage into the Family House.

3. They fight.

4. Enkidu wins Gilgamesh's consent to a draw.

iii

1. Gilgamesh craves adventure—to seek out and destroy Humbaba in the forest of evil. The beginning for the two rivals—now friends—of entering the forbidden, the threshold (marked by the possessive gods) of the quest for immortality. Enkidu tries to

dissuade him, sensing its danger—the danger of tampering with nature itself.

Enkidu encountered Humbaba before—his roaring is the flood-storm.

Enkidu tries to keep Gilgamesh from the adventure which will cause his own death.

2. The elders and the people encourage the fight with Humbaba, craving heroic action they lack.

3. The two friends visit Ninsun and hear her warning. Ninsun prays to the gods. She adopts Enkidu. She warns each to guard the other, tries in vain to tell her son of his friend's fate. The two vow loyalty.

iv

1. The journey into night (". . . the evening will find its way into me without me . . . " echoes in Joyce).

2. The digging of a well.

3. Enkidu encourages Gilgamesh, who is weakening. (The animal will.)

4. They arrive at the forest. Enkidu shrinks. Gilgamesh encourages him onward.

5. They arrive at the mountain. All is hushed.

v

1. Still, deep in their consciousness the mountain is familiar.

2. Gilgamesh awakes from a dream—of a mountain falling.

3. Enkidu thinks the dream of "the graceful man" is favorable.

4. In the morning Gilgamesh begins clearing the forest—the sacred trees. The enraged Humbaba comes. They fight. The monster-guardian is killed. Yet Enkidu warns it is not over.

vi

1. Gilgamesh's victory, bathing in the stream.

2. The goddess Ishtar, comes. She offers marriage and power . . . to Gilgamesh. He knows marriage with her would mean death and rule among the dead. He cites her victims to her face—animals, men. . . . He rejects her mortal diadems. She flies to her father, Anu (benign, detached), who agrees to let her inflict humankind with the Bull of Heaven (suffering, drought) for this insult, but asks that a little be stored by for the survival of these human servants to the gods. . . . The two friends have clearly gone astray and need the lesson.

3. Enkidu has a vision of the gods in council deciding one of them must die because they cut down the sacred cedars of the forest. Enkidu knows it will be he, not Gilgamesh, who is part god, the son of Ninsun, a goddess.

4. The gods decide. It is Enkidu. He recalls the "door" of the forest that was death itself, that lamed his hand, that gave the warning he disobeyed. It is now suspended before him.

He curses the harlot for making him come to this end. Gilgamesh says, "why do you curse? She made

97

you like a man."—"What is that?" Enkidu in his anger and despair asks.—"The world will mourn you," Gilgamesh promises.—"What is that?"

Gilgamesh will wander over the steppe in search of his friend's soul and bring it to peace, he promises. Enkidu recalls an old homeless man and weeps.

5. Enkidu dreams of his rival-friend's power over him. He visits the underworld of the dead, the sought for (in vain).

vii

1. Enkidu tells his already-grieving friend Gilgamesh he is a coward, that he can't bear this suffering.

2. Gilgamesh tells his friend he is brave, and reminds him of their vows to safeguard each other, always.

3. Gilgamesh sees Enkidu dying, cannot bear the evil that has risen from their victory to rob him of his friend, falls into hysteria.

viii

An interlude. Out of each death there is another movement—a further life—a quest renewed. The soul that is broken once by life may fear but cannot grieve its own death. (Echoes in Thomas's " . . . after the first death there is no other.")

Gilgamesh is terrified by shadows, the sight of an

animal, and yet in grief he puts on the skins of animals to be closer to his friend. He enters the road toward the mountains of Mashu. He encounters the scorpions (those at the end of the world, cf. Apocalypse) whose glance is death. Scorpion man and wife, deniers of what is beyond them of hope.

He journeys to find his (spiritual) father in his search for eternal life. He is always at thresholds of the forbidden.

Gilgamesh is told "go back to your city." He sees in the scorpion man only a guard whose heart is bitter and for whom he weeps but looks away. He must go on. It is his *vow*.

He enters the valley of tempting jewels he might have shared with his friend Enkidu. He speaks his name—"Enkidu." The loneliness now breaks his heart.

ix

1. "Why do you wander?" he hears from the alewife, whose cottage is by the sea. She takes him in though he is ravaged and wild with grief. Her offering is guileless and wise, but it threatens to separate him from the sorrow which binds him to his friend. (A woman first brought the friends together; a goddess bound them by vows; Ishtar took away his friend's life; now Sidhuri, the alewife, would separate him from his grief. He is wary of further loss.) She detects in his despair his deeper longing, though she says "you are in search of the wind." She tells him it is fruitful to stay with her and raise a

family, sterile and useless to go on: man's fate is death; only the gods have life. He must go on.

2. In mercy she tells him of the boatman Ur-shanabi and the waters of death that only he can cross.

3. He finds Urshanabi, who tells him: "I have lost all my care for the living." But he takes pity. He gives him a boat and poles. When the poles break, the boatman warns, he mustn't touch the water, but use only his mind—nothing will help.

4. The poles break on the hidden reefs. He makes a sail of his clothes. He drifts across the sea of death, arrives exhausted, weeps with his father.

5. The father tells him the truth.

X

1. The narration of the flood of Utnapishtim, his spiritual father—"The gods had chosen me; I did not know why."

2. The test of the loaves, of Gilgamesh's capacity to stay awake.

3. The old man Utnapishtim tells the weary journeyer—that is, under the prodding of his sym-pathizing wife—of the plant deep in the sea's garden.

4. Gilgamesh returns to the boatman; ties stones to his feet; descends into the water; seizes the plant; his hands are cut by its barbs.

5. He cuts loose the stones; the sea casts him up on the shore.

6. He tells the boatman he is going to take the plant to Uruk to bring Enkidu back to life (or, to give

to Uruk all that it asked him to bring: eternal life in its soul).

7. He journeys homeword and rests, sees a well whose water is fresh and cool. He strips and descends into it to bathe. A serpent comes and carries the unguarded plant away, leaving behind only its slough.

I would be a fool if I were unable to confess the spiritual crisis under which I grope toward this retelling and its final internal resolution. Throughout the day. Until finally it became intolerable to bear alone. I went out to a café in the early evening. I sat alone at a small circular table sipping a cognac. At first I barely saw the clochard begging a few tables away from the sidewalk. Some young punk mocked him and then the clochard pulled up his sleeves and showed the brand marks of a German concentration camp on his wrist. The young French punk mocked him again and sarcastically scolded him for making a poor showing against the Germans. The clochard in a sudden burst of sober defiance and wrath, spat out "Merci! Merci!" and walked off.

Late that night I woke, having dreamt that *Gilgamesh* and *Enkidu* were branded on my wrists, though I knew immediately the clochard's suffering was of another order far greater than my own. I remembered my own early experience of loss at my father's death and the bankruptcy that followed, two brands never left behind, anticipating others, but none of the same atrocious order.

In the morning (July 11) I read a bit of the *Iliad*. The poet's cry: "Sing Goddess wrath . . . " to pierce

101

one's heart and then the others' violently before attaining serenity. I felt defeated. I feel defeated still. There is a madness in storytelling and retelling and a cry that is thrown out at the sea. If the cry is not torn from one's own heart by what one sees and feels, it is not a cry at all. My legs have been like jelly for hours. I leaned out my window for a glimpse of something else and I looked minutely at the vines clinging with tiny sucking shoots to the stone, each bearing the enormous weight unto itself, their pale green leaves hanging breathless in the warm still air.

July 12—Visit with Louis Massignon in his study. I waited in his living room for forty-five minutes while he spoke first with two other visitors, one a Moroccan communist, he later told me, the other a young priest-to-be. The concierge told me on my way in (I have become familiar enough for her confidences apparently) that many come to her door asking to see the professor but few have the courage to go up. When we were at last together he railed against injustice, particularly injustice against the lowly. He told me he has made a vow—at seventy-six—that if a certain Algerian who is wanted by both the French police and the Algerian terrorists comes to the Muslim-Christian pilgrimage in Brittany later this month and is arrested, he will enter prison with him. It is incredible, I thought; it is mad.

At times I feel like Melville's Ishmael signed on the Pequod, yet the captain's wound is internal, his motivating power is not revenge; he is hostly, he is not reclusive; he is open, he is not secretive; he seeks the overthrow of every evil, one by one, not merely in general. . . . He told me today that he feels sometimes he is Don Quixote.

July 13 – Brief visit with Pierre Gabrier to go over some more of my translation. He was in a foul mood because his son Jean accidentally broke an antique chair that belonged to a grandmother. He said bitterly to his son, "Your dead brother was never so clumsy!"

I believe his immediate family members – his wife, son, two daughters – have such dark circles under their eyes from his loving only his dead son and their having to enter the world of the dead in order to find his love. His wife, a blunt and normally happy, unbrooding woman, I think, tells him off and on, "You are a beast, Pierre." It mellows him for a moment. I know he'll turn full force on me when he discovers my continuing friendship with Massignon.

Pierre quoted Claudel sensitively, saying that "the first kiss is not a thing rehearsed but awkward and pure – the kiss of God the same."

A touching line, but too much obsession with innocence and purity for me. Pierre lapsed into another obsession, railing about "the Russian and Chinese overruning my beloved violated and virginal France, destroying the church and killing my wife and children." His eyes blazed forth with his pseudo-prophetic nightmare. "The Algerians are their agents – torturers, rapists, murderers, heathen forerunners of Satan!"

If St. Bernard were to arise and preach his Second

Crusade all over again, Pierre would go with all his venom on his sword. He's a lunatic. Yet he's also so gifted. In him there seems no correlation, no way of linking to the world but through rage.

Later in my local café, just off rue Guynemer, I read some pages of Gertrude Stein, who owed much, she said, to children, to their fundamentally honest, astonished minds: Why does John's dog refuse to eat? Yes, why, indeed? Ignazio doesn't like to study and when others read he hides under the table. Yes, he does.

I felt freed.

What is a mosquito doing above the light?

Why does Erten have a birthmark on her cheek and neck?

Why did Charlotte Jones die so young that no one has remembered her until they're older and have their own grief?

Do only the aged's deaths "release us a little," as said Santayana, whom Gertrude Stein commemorated once at his birthplace in Avila?

Brittany, July 24—Early today, at Binic, in Professor Massignon's summer house, he sat me down at his writing table beside him and said "let's to work. We have a long road to go together, though mine is nearly over." He told me various languages I must learn, a fellowship I should seek, a university position I should have. . . . I knew he was seeking a disciple at this point and I knew I was not a disciple, if for no other reason than my age and my lack heretofore of linguistic preparation. He sensed my chagrin and embarrassment, leaned back a little in his chair, and said "You are a poet. You understand the transpositions from one language to another that the illiterate doesn't understand." It seemed a veiled insult or, at least, a shy admission of disappointment. I recalled Don Quixote's sidekick Sancho Panza. Am I the only fool available for this mad journey together? He will have to tell me how to do everything, since I know nothing about what he's doing, and he will have to repeat it, because a fool is stupid even about what he knows. On the other hand, if I am foolish enough to go along, I am also perhaps wise enough in my skepticism to keep him tied to the earth a little while longer and detached enough to find my way alone when his has ended. What else have I planned for my time anyway?

Paris, July 31 — The Muslim-Christian pilgrimage in Vieux Marché, near Plouaret, came and went July 25–26, without incident. Quiet, serene. Recitation of the *Fatiha* verses of the Qur'an in the small Dolmen crypt beneath the Chapel of the Seven Saints. Melkite Rite mass in the chapel above, the Muslim guests in the first two rows, the mass conducted by Mgr Nasrallah and his assistant priest from St. Julien le Pauvre in Paris. Night procession to the *tantad* (bonfire) around which was recited a Breton *Gwerz* ("epic poem") about the building of the chapel "before the world began." The next day: visit to the "holy spring" with its "seven sources," once known for its cure of blindness. Afterwards a "meal of Abraham," lamb and couscous, with dancing and singing and storytelling, a grand occasion of reunion. Bretons, North Africans, Parisians, others. The

105

Breton women's white coiffs rocked like sails in the anonymous darkness toward the *tantad*.

August 2—Visit to St. Julien le Pauvre. Mgr Nasrallah was conducting a mass with his assistant. Afterwards I ate some breakfast in a *salon du thé* near Notre Dame. An exhibition of paintings in the *salon* attracted my eye. Some were woodcut in quality— primitive, simple, strong. Dino Cavallari, the painter's name. Strong deep earth colors. Evoked the Breton mood again. I asked the proprietor his address and immediately (audaciously) wrote a card asking to meet him and see more of his paintings. I never did anything like that before. For some reason I believed he would be interested in Gilgamesh.

Received a letter from Professor Massignon with a press cutting about the pilgrimage, a response to my note of gratitude following those three days. He wrote in English, a mixture of pen and type. (I had mentioned Gilgamesh; my father's older brother who was blind; the death of a college friend.)

[hand] My dear friend,

Your letter alone would help me to hope, in this dark hour of my dear country, so fearfully heartless. Two things,—the pilgrimage for the sake of a friend's resurrection,—and light borrowed from blinds.

(as for blind,—my right eye has lost 9/10 of its strength,—and my left is daily decaying)

Friendship is vowing towards immortality, it doesn't know the passing away of beauty (take care),—because it aims towards the Spirit.

106

51 years ago I built my new life of Faith in urging Our Lord to take out of Death (of sin) the friend who had led me (indirectly) through his sin, – to eternal Love: teaching me in a crooked way, – that love was to surrender, to be wrung from our inmost heart, – so as to have only in mind His will, not mine.

[type] You have understood that what interests me in this life, is to find the Well of Immortality, as your Gilgamesh; and, in a rather extraordinary way, the VII Sleepers were shown to me by this extraordinary mystic, Hallâj (crucified for love in Baghdad, in 922 of our era = in 309 of the hegira) by the year of his death, 309 h., which is *exactly* the number of the Sleep of the Seven in Ephesus according to the Qur'ân (chapter 18). Hallâj said he would quicken the Seven from their sleep by his crucifixion, – and it seems he left me that task after 1000 years; because I published his "Tâsîn" (which, in arithmology is 300 + 9 = 309) in 1913, and had my main work ("Passion d'al-Hallâj") received in the Sorbonne in 1922, the trial of Hallâj having begun in 913, and ended in 922. (I am joking.)

The only goal: is to make the Dead get out of the grave, and this implies taking prisoners out of their jail, and sinners out of their sin. I think that love's kiss kills our heart of flesh, – it is the only way to *eternal* life, which should be unbearable if among the dying flowers, and the shrieking farewells of the over-stretched arms of our spoiled hopes. I think Compassion is God's pure act which burns forever, and be it in Heaven or in Hell doesn't matter for me; because Hell is the everlasting gift of His presence to the lonely heart who is longing amidst perishing fantoms, and doesn't care to find any immortality if not in the pure loneliness of the Holy One, this loneliness which the Holy Trinity enjoys forever, inside (and *outside*) of the glory of His attributes, and of His creation. Hallâj said, on the cross: "it is enough for the ecstatic to find his Only-One singled in Himself." And that is the cup of immortality.

Brotherly to you,
[hand] Louis Massignon

August 3—One of my young tutees, Eliso, from Madrid, age nine, said today in an alert moment that Gertrude Stein would've admired: "the Siamese kitten never forgets those he loves." Eliso otherwise yawns when I try to get him to study.

I wrote Thomas Merton about Massignon, the Breton pilgrimage, other things.

The American army officer who lives across the street erupted in the night, screaming, smashing glass. A French woman lives with him. They have a little girl, five or six years old. I think they've left him. He's been screaming and cursing for several days and nights, intermittently. His voice echoes up and down the street and draws people to their windows. Tonight the police came, six in a black van; two with machine guns slung over their shoulders. Everything became silent. They went into the building, then came out again and left. His cries resumed, low moans like a wounded animal's then intensified, followed about an hour later by silence.

Unable to sleep I read some St. John of the Cross—himself. I was reading, as always, for his "path," comparable in some sense to the Buddhist, the Taoist, the Sufi "paths of Life," seeking from him an answer to "how to live?" after asking laboriously "who am I?" and "what do I really want?" Is there a Christian mystical "path"—a serious and sound one, that is—that is not reserved only for clerical experts?

I considered "the ten steps of the mystic ladder of Divine Love" ("this ladder of contemplative purgation") (contrast the Buddhist Eightfold Path):

1. Causes the soul to languish ("if you find my Beloved, tell Him I am sick with love").

"In this sickness the soul swoons as to sin and as to all things that are not from God, for the sake of God Himself."

The soul "finds not pleasure, support, consolation or abiding-place in anything whatsoever."

2. Causes the soul to seek God without ceasing. ("I *will* rise and seek the One Whom my soul loves.")

3. Causes the soul to work and gives it fervor so it will not fail. ("Love teaches one how much is due the Beloved.")

4. Causes in the soul habitual suffering because of the Beloved, yet without weariness.

Christ grants the soul "joy" here and visits it, succouring it.

Jeremiah: "I have rmembered you, pitying your youth and tenderness, when you went after me in the wilderness."

In the absence of rest and quiet, desire burns to ascend further.

5. Causes the soul to desire and long for God impatiently. The step of "hunger."

Every delay becomes very long, amidst delusions of finding the Beloved before He is found. The lover believes he must see the Beloved or die.

6. Causes the soul to run swiftly to God and touch Him again and again; it runs without fainting to reason of its hope. The heart (charity) is greatly enlarged within it.

7. Causes the soul to become vehement in its boldness and daring. "Delight" in the Beloved.

8. Causes the soul to seize Him and hold Him fast without letting Him go—for short periods of time only.

9. Causes the soul to burn with sweetness. The purified, the perfect union with God.

10. Causes the soul to become wholly assimilated to God by reason of the clear and immediate vision of God which it now possesses; the soul passes beyond the flesh.

In this last step of the secret ladder nothing remains hidden. The Divine Essence consumes the soul. "For love is like fire. . . " The soul wears the white of faith, the green of hope, the purple of charity to protect it on its journey from its adversaries and enemies, the world, the Devil, and the flesh.

In white the soul journeys invisible to Satan. In green the soul sees the things of the world as dry and faded, dead and valueless, drawn only to external life. In purple the soul goes forth from itself in the dark night and from all things created "kindled in love with yearnings. . . ."

Above all, the soul desires union with God. That is the secret in the heart.

The last chapter of the *Dark Night* evoked a childhood house of terror: the living room where disembodied hands lifted drinks and mouths opened to overabundant meals; the bedrooms where souls lay on feather beds awaiting everything to come casually into them; the kitchen where the cleavers hung; the attic where the child hid from abandoned mirrors, naked, knowing nothing of the three garments and the threatening unholy disguises, desiring nothing, performing childish perversities to himself. The house of my sins, neo-Victorian, pseudo-Colonial, a mishmash of misunderstood designs, in which I discovered the truth could be empty. Where I once broke a swinging crystal chandelier to gain attention when the house was completely empty. Where my father once lay in state. And the river: the soul walked from the house to the river's edge, to the waters of the dead, where the mysterious darkness like a giant anaconda up from its ledges at night, lay its head on the shore, watching the wanderings of the spiritual child as he rushed to carry life down to the dead.

The secret path is a path of terror unless there is a blind guide to note the colors.

I thought of Gilgamesh and the alewife Sidhuri, their "duet": she saying "O you are chasing the wind" and he, unaware she is prefiguring the spiritual truth that is to come, "I will go on."

Such an epic must take form in the circular movement of one's spiritual life. One must pray with it to attain its spontaneity and simplicity—until it will begin and return of itself.

111

August 4 — Some misgivings the morning after due to my uncertainty about two things: both the Eight-fold Path and the Ten Steps: the one encouraging the cooling down, the other the heightening of desire; the one aiming at serenity, the other ecstasy, result ideally in compassion (I'm not sure how). Both, the one believing in the absence of union, the other in the totality of union, lay claim, as it were subtextually, to the virtue of balance (how is it achieved?). The way to the goals of compassion and balance in both cases, however opposite they seem, lies in the absence of obsession about either and in the overcoming of the erroneous self, the one through immersion in nothingness, the other in God. But what do I know?

Nemo scit utrum amore an odio dignus sit.

Furthermore, time seems to hang on the poet, as Yeats says, like a tattered robe, only on the saint like nakedness.

August 17 — A letter from Massignon in Binic dated August 13, written after his return from an International Congress in Denmark. He refers to August 13 as the "Ninth of Âb among pious Jews who mourn and fast for the two destructions of Jerusalem (Nebuchadnezzar's and Titus's) and recite the CL Psalms."

Today I have said the CL Psalms turned by the spiritual glance towards the Wall of Tears, where I have so often prayed (for the last time on Jan. 28, 1959). Strangely enough the very ground on which you must stand to pray before the Wall (ouside the Haram of the

El-Aksa Mosque) belongs to a "waqf" (pious Muslim foundation) of Tlemcenian Algerians (refugees from Spain since the XIVth Century), and since 1948 I have induced the French government, responsible for this foundation for poor Maghribi pilgrims, to pay (between 2 and 6 million francs annually) for maintaining the waqf. I inspect it personally every year, with an Inspector, an Algerian Muslim; in 1955 and 1956, he was this professor from Setif, my friend Hajj Lounis Mahfoud, who founded (or renewed) with me the devotion to the VII Sleepers, and who was killed on June 5th, 1957. I strongly believe that this waqf being "indivisible" from the Wall of Tears, is the cornerstone for the Jewish-Muslim reconciliation; and as soon as 1949, with the French Consul General in Jerusalem, we had begun to try to enable (but the Jordanian Govt. was obdurate and unjust) the Jews to come and pray at the Wall on the Ninth of Âb. Next year do say the CL Psalms on that day as I did this very year.

Yours brotherly,
Louis Massignon

I wrote a letter to Gabrier, who is vacationing in Brittany (not near Binic). I was responding to a pious poem called "Flagellation" he wrote and sent me:

"un poème est une petite voie à la liberté d'ésprit—surtout quand sa source est cachée et il y révèle beaucoup des portes d'entrée, dans les images. . . .

"Votre poème a une porte cachée, une prière d'une âme tendre et fragile qui voudrait faire un mot simple et spontané (comme on fait à la bien-aimée), mais il y a seulement un cri répèté. C'est le sens de l'en-

113

nemi que l' empêche et l'attachment à la pureté
(l'absence d'image) que fait la liberté impossible."
But I didn't send it, of course.

We ask who we are, what are our gifts, where
should we be, how should we live, incessantly until
we are chosen to do something we know, are inspired to do it, right where we are with the means at
our disposal.

Through Arnold Smit a visit with a chubby,
bouncy Dutch priest, Father Thiessen, who was on a
brief stopover in Paris on his way to Rome. He is a
Passionist father, a linguist (Latin, Greek, Hebrew,
French, English, German, Spanish, Italian, Dutch),
and a swift judge of people's concerns and interests.
We met on a street near l'Odéon and talked exhaus-
tively *in situ*. He had a book by Newman, whom he
praised for "balance." He was pleased I knew his
friend Daniélou ("he's daring"). He said Mauriac and
Bernanos had too many traces of Jansenism and obsessed too much about sin. He said Massignon was
"a genius" ("absolutely amazing gifts once for
discovering and reading texts"). At the end he said to
me in parting, "so, be yourself," and hurried off.

August 27—A conversation with Père Henri
Cazelles, Massignon's nephew, in his study at the Institute Catholique on rue de Vaugirard. Mostly about
Gilgamesh and what he called "the effortless vision
of human civilization running through the story: the
anger at his corruption by the people of Uruk—their
need for heroism—their sending their king out on a
hopeless voyage to conquer evil—their king being

114

heroic but tragically unequipped to carry the plant back to them: in a deep sense their fool." And a bit about Indian philosophy ("the essence of intuition") seeing human life directly, its nature—as opposed to its dialectic. He spoke of the Chinese and Mexican civilizations—"their aged wisdom." He came back to Gilgamesh: "it is a real picture of life before death, not a prophesy of purgatory. This unknowing of what's to come is very deep and crucial in the story."

This sense of unknowing of Utnapishtim given immortality without knowing why; Gilgamesh given impatience, a tragic gift for him, for there is in it no sense of hope, only heroic determination; he loses the plant, and we are never told why. Intuitively we know he must, but what do we know? It may be, it may not be. The ambiguity is not our typical professional intellectual's playfulness with options. It is much deeper. It is the depth we must fathom and where the secret of the story and its inspiration for retelling lies. And once seized, it will be lost again. "You must know that depth to tell of it."

I walked alone afterwards for hours through the Paris streets, noticing nothing of the city, seeing only the story unfolding scene by scene, feeling the terrible sorrow of Gilgamesh for his friend Enkidu, hearing Gilgamesh's promise to give his friend a royal funeral; feeling tears burst from his eyes and, deeper, feeling the knot inside his stomach, his guts, at the inexplicable death of friendship, and the desperate desire and vow to keep his friend alive; crying out to Utnapishtim to give the secret, hearing the old man's wife say "Give him the secret—he has suffered so."

115

August 29—I visited Mlle David, a French scholar who has worked on Gilgamesh, in her small apartment near the Sorbonne. Père Cazelles had insisted that one must not use this epic in a polemical way, and now I am reminded why. Mlle David finds in the story not a tragic poet's vision but the affirmation of the perfect man who through his own heroism overcomes the animal in man. She attaches much polemical (even political) hope to this: to his ability to create his own destiny. My own contrasting perspective dates to my own first reading, in 1954, when I was struck deeply by the poet's vision of the irony of human life, the faultiness of human thinking, and the piercing attachment of the human heart. It is a heroic epic in the formal sense of the hero's bombast, fighting scenes, impossible undertakings, and the rest; but the hero's flaws are always apparent and the poet has no illusions drawn from a more glorious past to feed his audience. The human tragedy is paramount as it is in Sophocles and Shakespeare, stripped even more in its basic nobility of spirit than theirs. For Mlle David, if I understand her in conversation and in her published article correctly, the Gilgamesh *idea* is a dialectic, not a story. But, then, she also believes that Bacon authored Shakespeare's plays.

August 30—There is a tradition that an epic precedes a drama: the epic is the real vision of a civilization's interior condition projected whole; the drama is the crisis of that civilization lived in each man's heart. Perhaps the sequence is reversed for us now, given our quite proper insistence on particulars

116

and, as a consequence, our quite natural anxiety in the face of universalizing metaphors. Yet metaphor there will be, and it will not come merely as the result of accumulation of particulars. It will come, as it has for every civilization, through deep feeling and simple grasp of what evokes that feeling most profoundly.

August 31—Notes arrived today from T. Merton and L. Massignon, both in anguish:

(excerpt) Merton: "When it is dark, it is dark, and you go in the dark as if it were light. *Nox illuminatio mea*. The darkness itself is our light, and that is all. The light remains, simply, our every day mind, such as it is, floating on a sea of darkness. . . . Tell your friends there to pray for me because I need prayers at the moment."

(excerpt) Massignon: "Mme Chauffin is in a great trial. Pray for her. . . . The 'rescue' of our ultras by the racists of Australia, South Africa, etc., in the Algerian question, makes me shudder. Sodom has been doomed, not for unnatural crime, but when they asked of their guest Lot to surrender his Guests, so as to abuse God's Angels. What are we doing with the 'regrouped Muslim women and children,' graciously put under the care of our soldiers, to 'mend their morals' and induce them to love our stick and whip? My dear country is getting 'possessed' by evil spirits. And the cowardice of our Cardinals and Bishops keeps me awfully in AWE."

September 2—On the positive side Merton also said (excerpt): "One of the most fascinating things I have

117

had my hands on in a long time is that offprint of Louis Massignon about the Seven Sleepers. It is tremendous, and I want to know more about all those places and things. Especially the dolmen. . . . How would you like sometime at your leisure to do into English the Breton *Gwerz*?"

Which I mentioned to L.M. on the phone late yesterday and to which he responds in a note just received today (excerpt): "Dear Friend, Henri Cazelles is not only an exegete but a man. As for Thomas Merton, I must provide him with all four parts of my technical study of the Seven Sleepers printed by Geuthner. Give me his address, which I need to thank him. I think Mme Chauffin has given to the VII two very high supporters, your friend Merton, through you, and Cardinal König of Vienna" Signed, "Yours friendly (in Gilgamesh and Enkidu)."

September 3 – A montage: Monique, a secretary who lives across the hall, came back from vacation in Spain with a rash on her chin which she has painted with a pink powder. She is usually smiling and now she is forced to be serious. Unlike the woman in the boulangerie with the enormous set of false teeth who is grumpy but is forced to always smile. I smell baked potatoes and hear the glass cutter in the street below – a sharp, almost squealing call; several panes of glass in a case strapped to his back and bending him over, like Atlas holding up a transparent building. There is a small boy across the street on a very high balcony that has chicken wire around it. He's looking down at me and I'm waving up. When I stop reading poetry, I forget everything but the

118

spirits of poets. Even less than do Lot's angels, they have nothing hostly then enabling them to enter the city. Thoughts in the boat, drifting on the waters of the dead, on a voyage that knows no other side. The wind has ceased. Becalmed. The shirt I've tied to the remains of an oar hangs down like half an empty body clung to wood. He who dreamed of stars to be read and of mountains to be scaled, silent and im-mobilized. Who bathed at the sacred wells that cure the blind, tired of the boat's stillness on the stagnant sea inside himself. The broken oars, the dry eyes, the dip upward of the green liquid in an absinthe glass touching an old concierge's lips.

September 6—Pierre Gabrier appeared at my door unexpectedly this evening. He sat down in the "liv-ing room" part of my small flat. I fixed some coffee and offered some pastry, which he refused. He seemed very agitated and his first words—since he has no small talk like "how are you"—were a harangue against the modern world, the materialism of Americans, all the familiar and obvious things I knew were not what brought him to visit me. Slowly he began to inquire about my friendship with Massignon. With alarm in his face more than words on his lips he conveyed an attachment to me I had not suspected. I think I had actually come to be something of a poor replacement for his dead son. He told me that he had gone to Massignon after his son's drowning and asked him if his son was in Heaven. Massignon, he said, told him "no one can be sure where the soul goes or if it has any value at all or exists. . . ." Even the diction (in French) was

119

uncharacteristic of Massignon's sometimes herky-jerky, elaborative, digressive style, but I said nothing. My silence disturbed him greatly. He said suddenly, "I want to warn you against him. He told me himself that he had once committed the sin of Sodom." I said nothing. It seemed to me none of my business. He stood up and walked to the door. His eyes were at the point of bursting into tears, of humiliation and rage, not grief, and I wanted to tell him none of it mattered to me and we were still friends, but he left with neither of us saying anything more.

After he left I felt heaviness all around. Grief. Un-naturalness. Death. Loss. The weight of his son's loss upon him. His terrible yearning for purity.

I hated being placed between these two men. I could feel time running out for me in France, regardless of how long I actually stay. I feel indebted to Pierre for introducing me through his book to St. John of the Cross. I feel indebted to Massignon for a generosity not so clearly determined.

News earlier that Père Jean de Menasce has suffered a paralytic stroke in Geneva and has not regained his speech. Yvonne Chauffin phoned me. She also said she's trying to find me "une situation" in Paris with a publishing friend. But I know all this must come to an end, if I believe the poem of "the reader of hearts" (al-Hallaj), that the Secret of my Friend I came to find must be buried with me in my inmost soil, watered from the cups of serving maids in order for a new and sacred plant to grow in seven days.

September 7—I made a rather bizarre configuration of the "secret steps" and the cliché "house of cards"

120

stimulated by Mlle David's note this morning about the serpent's eating the plant that Gilgamesh left unguarded *"comme il faut."* It suggests, I'm not sure to what end, a negative "path of life" through necessary losses.

The first room of the house of cards is Sodom and the tendency toward any inward perversity derived from excess or loss of personal attachment.

The second room is the seemingly inextricable fear of death for oneself, an animal fear.

The third room is the readiness of argument born of cowardice, a deprivation of spiritual liberty in oneself and its denial to others: a need of patience in the rooms.

The fourth room holds one in fear of darkness, fear to descend the stairway to the room below that is filled with moonlight and a black shadow around its edges.

The fifth room is the fear of invasions of what one holds delusively in private. It is the room of perpetual introspection.

The sixth room is the room of isolation and manufacture of false lights.

The seventh room is the room of entertainment of Satan in a *danse macabre*, the handholding of the living with the dead, the sensual grasp of the fragile fingers on one's spoiled hopes, the penultimate perversion.

The eighth room, which few experience, is the room of emptiness, where we scramble up through the antennae on the roofs of our hellish cities and we begin to fly out of our tangled metal forests, out of all false communication.

I recall Baudelaire's *Benediction* (excerpt): "Et dont les yeux mortels, dans leur splendeur entière,/ Ne sont que des mirois obscurcis et plaintifs!"

I think I am not in Paris but Uruk, at least in my mind.

Yvonne phoned late. I confided my being put in the middle by Gabrier's jealousy. She said she learned painfully that "death is death; it demands a release." She said Pierre risks loss of his faith and his reason by refusing to release his son's death. She said that his crisis which colors his whole worldview stems from the fact that before his son drowned in Lake Geneva they had quarreled over something quite banal and he doesn't to this day know if his son drowned from despair or by accident, since he was an excellent boatsman and swimmer.

She spoke again of my "situation." "Bifteck, sans crise, est très bon pour l'inspiration."

I wrote a brief note of appreciation to Mlle David for sharing her article. I reaffirmed what Eliot has made clear, that there is a vast region of interdependence between the poet and the scholar, especially as long as each resists the temptation to draw the other's conclusion.

September 9—A letter from T. Merton dated Sept. 3 arrived this morning (excerpt):

The main purpose of this immediate reply is that I want to say how deeply moved I am at this idea of Louis Massignon's that salvation is coming from the most afflicted and despised. This of course is the only idea that makes any sense in our time. It is the key to our time or to any other time. It is the great idea of the Bible, the Prophets, everything. I have been obsessed with it for a long time, and this picture has something to do with it. It is not a very good photograph, lacks all contrast and all light-and-shadow. It is of a statue of the Bl. Virgin I had done for the novitiate by a sculptor in Ecuador. The idea is precisely that of Louis M. The Holy Mother is the Indian woman of the Andes, the representative of all that is most abject, forgotten, despised and put aside. The artist, who is a bit of a leftist if not a red, caught on to the idea very well, and the face of the Mother is terrific. It has precisely the kind of blindness, the withdrawnness in a great mystery of poverty and darkness and strength. There are barely any eyes at all. It is like a rock, and yet warm and full of life. As for the child, however – the Christ, the Resurrection to be born from the despised peoples of Mexico and the Andes – He is full of joy and triumph and holds in His hand a completely mystical bit of fruit invented by the sculptor, which is the only lively and ornate thing in the whole work and is very effective: it is salvation.

I wanted you to see this thing, beautifully done in mahogany from the jungles of South America, and carved in the Andes, with the spirit of the Andes and of the peoples who live here. It expresses something with which I am very much concerned and for which I ask many prayers. It makes me able to tell you that I am in complete solidarity with you and Louis Massignon on this point and that I want badly to go ahead, as God may permit, in somewhat the same direction, but over here.

123

Your account of Gilgamesh is tremendous. I will have to get the epic. I had heard of it of course in connection with Genesis. I will be rereading your poem in the light of the summary you send and will write more about it later. I just wanted to get this picture into the mail for you and Massignon. By the way, I want to put something about Hallaj in the book I am writing, and have nothing at hand. Can you lend or send me anything? The book is all about inner experience, intuition, the inmost self that sees in and through our whole being, and not just through intellectual constructions – which too often are a veil between us and experience, deliberately woven to frustrate immediate experience . . .

God bless both you and Louis – thank you for your words on my Pasternak article. Here is another offprint that just came in.

Faithfully and affectionately in Christ,
Tom

September 13 – Liberty may finally be the effortless ability to listen and be joyous at the discoveries of another.

September 23 – A visit with Massignon in his study. He looked old, his eyes looked weak, tonight. He said cryptically: Claudel said there is one thing worse than being deceived: having the self given the things it wants.

He talked about the desert – the coldness at night; the possibility of being drowned suddenly in a downpour; the prayer of a downpour; the solitude. He

124

spoke of the Seven Sleepers' wells south of Vieux
Marché; the madman hallucinating mirrors around
himself in the desert; the end of matter by thought.
"We are such weak creatures," he said in an old,
almost tinny voice. I think he is a bit of an actor, an
exaggerator, like us all. "We feel the terror of truth—
that it comes in a destruction of ourselves—and we
desire it by loving it before we know the price it is
going to exact from us. It exacts from us the
strangest of things, which we cannot exact from one
another and expect to live: that we cease thinking of
the world through the eyes of those we love—that
we literally 'aim' towards the Spirit, the 'shadow'
behind the candle (which is suffering). That we cease
indulging our sorrow over a world devoid of someone we love. The Father, for the sake of man, forgot
His Only Son, so that man could take Him in his
heart and carry that transfusion into others, throughout the intricate veins of humanity. The very form of
man is strange—and the weak, weak spirit inside him
is only weakened more by sudden fires. The secret of
humanity is found in the silent," he said, "especially
silent women."

He paused and we sat for awhile without speaking. Then he said. "You must not think our suffering
that comes when we are old and sick of ourselves is
the same as that of children or of Christ Himself,
God's only Son." He was silent again. Then he said,
"Because there are things we can't endure, why does
God prolong us so?"

Late at night, long after the visit, I realized that in
sharing another's depth, I may understand, but it remains his. I wonder if friendship is born of each

one's glimpse in the other of his own yearnings for joy.

October 1—Gabrier paid me another surprise visit but this time he came with the sole intent, he said, to read me several poems of Baudelaire, which he read beautifully from an elegantly bound volume, leaning back in the couch, seemingly calm. At the end, just before he left, he asked me if I'd seen Massignon again. I said yes. His lips trembled and he tried to hide his anguish in a smile. He embraced me in the doorway and said he hoped I liked his reading. I did. Earlier in the day I was handed bread in a boulangerie by a dwarf. Now, when life is strange, how else can we understand but to cry?

November 1—Books arrived in the mail from Massignon, his edited *Akhbār al-Hallāj* full of accounts of the mystic's life, the *Dīwān* of al-Hallaj's poems, and the tomes dealing with the Seven Sleepers. I read for hours.

The fog in Paris was thick today. Cold drizzles of rain. Late in the day I attended the opening of the exhibition of Sacred Art at the Musée Moderne with the artist Dino Cavallari, who told me "blue is the evocation of spirit—simple, pure—amidst the architectures of new harmonies." We walked among the works in silence, without needing to say anything or prove agreement or justify disagreement.

Late at night I thought Massignon was speaking, or did I dream his words that man might not be damned for sin but for his refusal to live with a broken heart—and Al-Hallaj's words that the Devil is damned for all the sufferings, watching suffering evolve salvation unable to drink of it. I sat up in bed seeing al-Hallaj dancing in his chains.

December 3 – A note from Massignon written December 1, the anniversary of Charles de Foucauld's assassination (in 1916). He wrote: "the Fascists in France have tried to trick me by sending me a Catholic bishop who was with Juin and the others. Juin has sent a letter to deGaulle threatening him. These men are desperate. And the worst thing, they are trying to keep colonialism alive by wearing the insignia (the cross and heart) of Charles de Foucauld, trying to make him stand as the saint of colonialism." The note was waiting for me on my return from a few days in Vézelay. He wishes to see me before he leaves for Cairo, Damascus, and Jerusalem December 13. He has gotten a letter from Merton he wants to share. He recalled two days he spent in Vézelay in 1911 "meditating in solitude."

December 5 – A brief visit with Daniélou and afterwards, a few doors down, with Massignon. Both had received letters from Merton, the latter's with an enclosed sort of Indian poem on wisdom (one of Merton's "transformations," so to speak, not a translation). Massignon gave me two more of his own offprints. He also suggested I call on an old friend of his in his absence, a Jesuit, Père d'Ouince, who he said was his spiritual guide during the Occupation.

He spoke of two friends: first, Claudel, referring to his description of the universe as a rose whose petals

127

are still opening and beyond the edges of which there is nothing, not even the scent. He said Claudel was a sculptural poet who began in prose but rarely, unlike Baudelaire, reached the inner rhythm that is true poetry. Claudel, he said, like a sculptor could not consider things infinite, but was a finitist, seeing only the ends, the limits, the fixities.

Second, Chardin, referring to a visit together once in New York when Chardin was gravely ill and fearful of dying away from France and of his, Massignon's, telling him it was his vocation to die in New York. Chardin, he said, was an optimist; he believed deeply in a movement toward Omega, which was for him the heart of Christ. Chardin felt we were moving on, constantly on—that the present was an unmeasurable time. That is very metaphysical, he said; perhaps not so human or mystical, though harmonizing in its way. On the other hand, Einstein showed that a straight line curves and returns to itself.

He told me he has found it difficult waking or rising, yet suddenly he simply gets up; he wonders if he can get up, then he does. "It shall be that way after death. And we shall return into His body.

"Matter is important, just as numbers are. Everything is built on numbers, as we know since Mendeleev's series and Planck's constant. But," he said, after mentioning Fibonaccis' series and Cantor's transfinite numbers and his Aleph, "I am not an arithmetic Teilhard de Chardin to attempt the 'reconstitution' of the cosmos on Cantorian theorems, and I humbly use whole (I mean 'integer') numbers, God's given numbers, as said Dedekind—the others are merely our human invention.

"We are corrupt in body, but Our Lord took our
body and it was pure. The incarnation tells us
nothing is to be despised. Despising echoes in
despair. God is liberty. We know it in His love. We
know it especially when we know our prison. At
times when we are ignorant of the prison, we think
we are free and we despise love; we mock; we are
like those who have grown old inside, losing joy,
risking something worse than death: the kiss of
death and damnation is for one to think anyone, no
matter who or what, is unworthy of liberation."

In the silence that followed I thought of something
Yvonne Chauffin told me once: of his visit to a
young woman dying in a Paris hospital. He pierced
through the visiting hours screen and sat with her.
She came out of unconsciousness to recognize him
and tried to raise her hand to him (he kissed it) and
said "au revoir." "Oui," he replied, "au revoir." In
the grayness of hospitals I know there is no sentimentality in that.

He speaks of others as if he himself were a
stranger. He says this is the strange joy one knows
as one grows older.

He spoke of steps or rather "hops": that somehow
life was taking jumps for him—sudden thrusts, in-
stantaneous movements forward: "we note changes
suddenly."

"I feel old and weak yet lighter," he said.

When I stood up to leave he embraced me. His
hands felt like what I imagine Abraham's hands must
have felt like to those he received as guests.

"Visit Père d'Ouince," he told me, "with the same
simplicity."

December 12—Visit with Père d'Ouince. Tall, thin, calm. Massignon had told me this priest had been imprisoned and tortured by the Germans. His eyes are dark and deeply lined, seeming to look out through shadows into light. He asked me of my "itinéraire" (meaning experience). I had nothing similar to offer. His patience and attentiveness seemed almost unnatural (I am hesitant to say super-natural, for I don't know what this means) or other than normal. He seemed to absorb and harmonize the apparent plainness of the receiving room—the wooden table, the two straight chairs, the colorless walls—with his very fragility.

In contrast I discovered I harmonized little, perhaps nothing. I remember reading Ste. Thérèse's way of encountering the terrible grating of another's prayers, "harmonisé" somehow. But I was horrified by the cruel effects of his experience still visible upon his face and hands.

He stared at me a moment of extraordinary still-ness after I had had a rush of words. He said, "Per-haps you will write in solitude something that will touch the interior of the public. Maybe two or three things. Then gradually stop, for the most profound work will not be popular nor will you know its reward."

I asked him if he knew Gabrier's book on St. John of the Cross I had been translating now for over a year. He said quietly "it is a *vulgarisation* of St. John of the Cross." Painfully I had come more and more to the same conclusion. Mystical love seen under the tortured eyes of personal grief can be made mon-strous, can in fact select only what is monstrous to

130

explore and exploit. This is one realm—mystical love—that must be hidden from "use." For in personal grief, for instance, the "épreuve" is indeed unbearable and the mortification of self can be almost enjoyed. It is a poet's, not a mystic's, book. Perhaps poets have less courage and discipline than mystics when they encounter truisms in actual experience. The poet seeks to build a bridge to an audience for his discovery, the mystic accepts the chasm in obscurity as it is.

I learned much from Père d'Ouince's words and from his silence.

December 15—Gabrier phoned and asked me to meet him in a café, not in either of our homes. I had to do some research at the Bibliothèque Nationale for a new translation I was undertaking and we agreed to meet in a small café we both knew in the Marais district. We had coffee and some pastry and he told me of a new novella he is working on which, he said, is a kind of synthesis for him: a dialogue in a church between a young intellectual "penseur" priest and a clochard who has come in to sleep after having hurt his leg in a fall. The clochard was the rich man who could not follow Christ and who, in fact, "killed" his son who had intentions toward the priesthood. The drama is one in which the priest is forced to encounter despair: the profound theme of a father's "murdering" a son who is "poorer" than he. The priest is poor; he has no history, no complication; he is empty, charitable, at peace with himself. The clochard brings his exhaustion into the church as his only offering.

131

He stopped. He said he goes from optimism to pessimism about the work. We said little more apart from – something new for us – pleasantries. Later on my walk home I went into the church of St. Séverin, Huysmans' church, and sat in the shadows for awhile along with two nuns (Sisters of Charity).

I suppressed until the evening what Gabrier had said to me apart from pleasantries and the account of his novella; that is, his droning again about Mauriac and Sartre (leaving Massignon out of the triumvirate for a change): more like literary gossip than criticism, though the line between the two is not clear to me. He said both are "méchants." He said (without personally knowing either) that Sartre is not friendly and can be dangerous with certain persons for he is deeply perverse; Mauriac is contradictory in other ways. I commented only on Mauriac's praise of Sartre to me. He laughed and recounted some of the negative things M. had said about S. in print. What strikes me as important in S., especially in the present-day context of France in which I find myself, is his focus "en bas." Besides, in this context who isn't in some way perverse? Gabrier confided that what he fears most for himself is "solitude sans fin."

What is the source of this ubiquitous perversity of which everyone speaks, writes, murmurs, indulges? The wars, occupations, displacements, forced exiles, murders – have they collectively left humanity twisted out of any normal shape, incapable of communicating with one another except unnaturally and illicitly? Is the answer that clear? Can we find company only in perverseness? Does perversity have its ecstatic moments that leave shadows after it imprisons, terrible

132

nights of terror in unnaturalness until for awhile it seems normality? No wonder poets find in mystical writings the guides through their dark nights without considering—without being able to consider—the distinction between authenticity and vulgarization of experience? Are only negative transformations occurring under the self-guidance of faulty thinking? Of course, it could occur also perhaps had there been no such wars, occupations, atrocities, etc., by anyone's simply replacing the guide with the self. Who is the guide? and when has the human context ever been devoid of the possibility of perversity under the guidance of faulty thinking? Somehow the beginning of the quest for true guidance must start with the questioning of contextual evidence for the possibility of its subtle transformation into personal excuse.

And what is true poverty of spirit? Certainly not propaganda.

December 24—St. Anselm says "I will not turn my eyes even if a whole creation cries."

But the poet turns his eyes at every florescence the world ignites, however artificial or strange or ugly or untimely or irrelevant it proves to be.

We know who we are by what compassion, not mere curiosity, guides us to see.

Merton sent me a recent book of his for Christmas called *Nativity Kerygma*, an odd-shaped book, four inches wide, about eighteen inches long: from nativity to resurrection.

Perhaps I am not overly "religious" if my main consideration after reading it on Christmas eve is not its celebration of the idea of transcendent oneness

133

and the joy one feels in the diversity of creation, in each tiny birth, but rather the world as it is, the repugnance of nationalism, and the sentimentality of internationalism.

The serpent devours the plant. For us it is the only way to understanding.

December 27—Reading Racine's *Phèdre* (roughly translated "Your grace makes me a criminal." "O my son, what hope have I killed in you!"). The scene between Phèdre and Hippolyte, just after the news of Theseus' death, is indeed unbearable.

As I am an amateur, my thoughts written here are idle and of no importance beyond companionship in solitude. To me, the play's passion and irony unfold like a trick of architectural perspective (like the coolly conceived ceiling in Rome's San Ignazio basilica, not through a multiplicity of conflicting characters and relationships, as in Shakespeare): through interiorly constructed dimensions, mathematically correct, along long alleyways through arches: suddenly each dimension reveals itself, but somehow without surprise. At times I find myself bending it, deliberately moving something out of place, vulgarizing it imaginally, just to endure it.

The Greek consciousness washes more vitally on my shore directly than through Racine's siphon. I need to look out again at its sea to understand the land with its suffering humanity, its fallible leaders, its wasted seed. It makes the "nuit obscure" plausible as an auditorium in which a poet can call upon Calliope to help him sing the story he is given.

December 30—Late afternoon with Dino and
Francesco in their studio. Francesco, now six, was
drawing on a pad on the floor around the feet of his
father, who was working on a large oil of the Last
Judgment. Dino has made a four-paneled frame for
his son's bed covered with frescoes—blendings of
abstract forms, line drawings of primitive animals,
and strong naturalistic human figures with arched
backs, suggesting Noah's Ark. There is a mixture of
quiet compulsion and dramatic simplicity moving
through all the work of his I've seen thus far.

Over an Italian aperitif he told me he had become
"calme" in character following the war, his release
from confinement by the Germans first and, later,
the Americans as a prisoner of war and prisoner-of-
war suspect respectively, and, finally, after two
operations for injuries. He told me that a medium
said he would nearly die twice but would recover.
He has six boxes of sculpture in the *sous-sol*, but his
health and the size of the apartment won't permit
him to do any more. One day maybe they will have
a larger place, he hoped. Meanwhile, he is not
anxious.

The entrance downstairs—19 rue Malte-Brun—is
dark. Impossible to find the light button and, if you
do, the light stays on about three seconds. Same on
the winding stairway. The building smells of the old
concierge's cats no longer cleaning themselves. Once
you enter the Cavallari's two small rooms, however,
the world becomes illuminated and large.

Two small paintings on wood caught my eye: One
of a man bent over looking at his hunting dog, the
other of a peasant woman walking past a tree. The

135

red of the hunter's coat and the faded red of the woman's apron, the brighter red of a bird's wing barely visible in the tree, the browns of the earth, the humor in the hunter's sinister black hat. He said an American woman from New York had recently asked him to paint two larger oils of these studies for her penthouse studio collection.

Being even less an art critic than I am a literary critic, I thus declare Picasso a *thematic* artist, Rouault an *apocalyptic*, Cavallari a *naturistic*. Picasso religious aesthetically, Rouault devotionally, Cavallari organically. Cavallari finds religion in nature (animals, trees, rivers, buildings, clay, soil, hats, fingers): everything is animate. He is not an ideologue or message giver like the other two nor an experimentalist like Picasso. He is in touch with forces moving in things; a kind of geologist who works in pigments mixed with water and oil and any other metals or minerals he can get his hands on. He is genuinely pagan, I believe, like a Breton druid out of the dolmen past. It will take time for him to be "discovered," because he is not easily recognizable like the other two; but he seems to have time even if he exists, for want of being "discovered," in an ever-diminishing space. The more he paints, the more he diminishes himself in his manageable space. He witnesses something rare in art: the calmness of the earth, the possibility of life without anxiety, the existence of a "way" outside time through communion with nature before time began. Yet his work is dramatic, more naturally so than that of the politically or theologically conscious dramas of the other two—to me. But the other two's very prominence in setting

136

the taste for our generation in aesthetics and theology of religious art will delay the discovery of Dino's work for a long time, I believe, because one has to *see* with more than the eye and the text to recognize his art; one has to see the movement of stones.

He told me, quite apart from the above, that he didn't like to paint men and women until they become fathers and mothers. The look in the eyes between his son and his wife, he said, was pure, simple, profound.

He doesn't talk about art in theories; he prefers to talk about family or nature. Things must exist before he can talk of them, and then for the most part he prefers to contemplate them, not to talk.

He likes painting animals, especially birds, butterflies, bison, dogs. One painting of Moses suggests by the strength of the head and upper body, even the arch of the back, the existence and familiarity of the "paradise" of animals, their kindredness, and their natural grace of movement, surrounding him.

I feel with Dino that I *see* "the universe" of woods and stars and light. One painting of Christ, a small figure standing with his companion John the Baptist at a stream with birds in a tree and a dog at their feet, is alive through kindredness; quieting, conclusive. The rhythm and simplicity owes much to Giotto perhaps, at least to pre-Renaissance painters, but is clearly his own contemplation. His self and times disappear before his art, which of course makes him less accessible than most contemporaries. He is hidden, perhaps even intimidated by the times that have confined and impoverished him. Perhaps these are the "operations" (of self and times) he has undergone

137

that have made him both reclusive and "calme."
Though his is a vision, a sensibility, a fathoming of
life beneath the surface, not an escape from himself
and the times. He teaches me much, in a different
way from Massignon, about Gilgamesh: especially
the need to de-aestheticize and de-theologize it; to
see it moving before "time" in its own ageless
simplicity of rhythm through earth.

He told me he knows of Massignon and may do a
painting of him in a mantle one day. He has read in
the papers of the Muslim-Christian pilgrimage and
has begun a few small studies of the Sleepers with
their dog in the Cave.

Dino's hands are strong; has a strong build; quiet
forceful features in his face; dark glimmering eyes; a
relaxed squinting, crinkling smile like his son's; tan
skin. His Italian egg and cream liqueur is powerful in
a subtly overtaking way: when I left I nearly toppled
down the stairs each time the light went off.

He teaches me that to do Gilgamesh I must
find/embrace at least one primary virtue and surrender to it—patience.

Later, I saw an aged woman on the street pushing
a child in a carriage: a blue kerchief on her head,
bent ankles, brown shawl, arched forward, looking at
the child. Dino's people.

December 31—A letter arrived this morning from
Merton dated Christmas eve (excerpt):

The other day I happened to have a chance to see
the old Shaker settlement near Lexington. Only buildings, of course, nobody there since 1910. It was sad

and moving. It was once an intense and rather wacky spiritual center, but I think it was very significant. The truth and simplicity of their handiwork remains to bear witness to something tremendously genuine in their spirit. For some reason it made a similar intuitive impression on me to that made by the story of the Seven Sleepers. The spirit of these people was very alive in their building—the one I went into, the only one I could get into—had a marvelous double winding stair coming out in the mysterious pale light of a small dome at the top of the house. The silence, light and effect were extraordinary. There were some empty rooms at the top of the house, and I went into them to taste the silence—sunlity windows, looking out on bleak fields and a huge lebanon cedar, with the wind in it. You would like the place.

January 2, 1960—Visit with Gabriel Marcel. He is having to buy or vacate his apartment. He both laments and is grateful for Mme. Abeille's raising the money for this. He hopes I have not been "pressed to contribute." I hadn't. He spoke of the pain in his legs, of age. . . . He seems to sleep when he listens; his eyes close, but he hears: a contrast to Massignon's open piercing eyes and tendency to foresee what one is going to say.

Gabrier phoned, said his novella is finished and now he must go to the south of France on his government inspection business. He voluntarily assured me Massignon was "completely mad," that he knew from his own inspection of prisons that no Algerians were held as prisoners who were not out-and-out criminals and that there was absolutely no

139

truth to the accusation of torture against those held legitimately. Only the Algerians commit atrocities, he said.

January 25—A postcard from Massignon in Jerusalem dated 1/20/60, saying "coming back. I pray with you here." The photo was of the ruins of the church of St. Anne.

January 30—Upon his return I saw immediately that his eye has had a blood vessel break. Nearly a third of one side of his face is purple and he seems weary. He said he is trying to choose the right time for an operation that he knows may leave him blind in one eye. He told me of his days in Cairo: in his old archaeological building which had been taken over by Egypt during the Suez crisis of three years ago. He stayed in his old rooms and study which he had fifty-two years ago, and roamed the building alone. He was the only Christian at the conference of Orientalists (Sir Hamilton Gibb, he said, was not asked, though he, Louis, asked them to invite him next year). He went on to Jerusalem, where he had a cell in a convent. One day he felt life nearly leave him—"the intoxication of age"—and cancelled his meetings. He felt he was dying—that it was the place selected. He had not visited the Holy Sepulchre yet, only the Wall of Tears and the place of the three angels and the place where Lot is believed to have been buried. A brother of the Charles de Foucauld order brought him pills and injections of vitamin C, and in a few days he was better.

He talked about death. He has often talked about

death since I have known him. And of atoning. Of
Heaven being without banquets for him, and then (if
there are) only an "instant" after unconditional surrender of his will; for he could not stand an eternity
of himself. He quoted al-Hallaj again, saying that in
love one stands beside the beloved taking on His
very form, having no form of oneself left. He read
me a passage from the sermons of Meister Eckhart
that echoed this thought of al-Hallaj's.

He said deGaulle's recent speech on behalf of
Algerian independence is providential. I could see in
his face a certain weight beginning to be lifted, but at
the same time a fatigue accompanying his return
from the world to himself. "Of course," he said,
"when the wealthy bankers in Paris realize they are
losing Algeria and its oil, there will be a last surge of
violence in the streets and it will cause much
suffering."

He said in a whisper that Eckhart had written of
"a love as strong as death." He said, "We have to go
to the certitude of our defeat. Our Lord was defeated, yet triumphant. And we have to go in
exhaustion."

At the door he gave me a personal copy of
Huysmans' book on Ste. Lydwine. He said it is the
deepest book he has ever read and certainly
Huysmans' most profound work. He said Huysmans
was not a man of prayer, but he was writing this
book inside his own suffering and it is deep.

February 1—Car horns everywhere in Paris, some
protesting, some supporting deGaulle's recent
speech.

141

I thought of Massignon's saying to me once about joy: a single possessiveness of it brings a "douleur" that can be met with prayer and love only. I thought of Yvonne's "la brûlure."

February 5—An unexpected person, David Ottoway, phoned at the suggestion of a mutual friend in Boston. He's a Harvard undergraduate. We met and walked around the Ile de St. Louis. He's a devouring listener. His interest is the global political scene, especially meetings of statesmen—deGaulle, Khrushchev, Ike, the rest. He's very clear in his presentation of the stage settings and the implications of such encounters. The walk was very relieving and hopeful. Ottoway may be only twenty-one (I'm not sure of his age), but he's very sharp, not arrogant, perceiving, not fearful, wise.

When we parted, I walked toward my *quartier* feeling drawn away by Gilgamesh's remorse over his own involvement in his friend Enkidu's death.

In the evening, reading *Ste. Lydwine*, I found a postcard from Maritain to Massignon sent from Belgium in 1924, and a death notice of Huymans (1907) including a quote from his book *En route*: "Seulement, ne vous y trompez pas, la conversion du pêcheur n'est pas sa guérison, mais seulement sa convalescence." (p. 285).

February 12—An extended phone conversation with Massignon, who phoned he said because he was too ill for a visit just now yet wanted to be in touch. He said he is losing interest in material things more and more—"except for this connecting phone," he

laughed. He said he finds life narrowing, but that he
has been asked to go on a "desperate call" to aid
someone in Damascus, an old Muslim historian
friend who had a son by a French woman—with
whom the man briefly lived. He believes the son to
be living in France and asks Louis to go to him in a
certain place. He said he can only go now on such
seemingly hopeless and unlikely errands of mercy.
He spoke of his own depression and remorse years
before over his continued sinning after his conversion, and of Claudel's letter to him telling him not to
torment his heart, for it is a heart that will belong to
others. He said he had been in touch recently with
deGaulle, who he said feelingly is a solitary man
whose daughter went mad and died in Colombey-
des-Deux Églises, where he now lives. This daughter
is the sole light of his life and he has given the
money from his books for a hospital in her memory
there and prays solitarily by her grave. He is close to
nearly no one.

I felt the tiredness in his voice but he assured me
he wanted to talk. He said he had just received from
Merton his *Selected Poems*. He said he couldn't judge
the verses' merit but they showed he was a poet
rather than a dry theologian. He said he had
misunderstood him from some of the latter kind of
tracts he wrote. "One day God will take poetry from
him for he enjoys it so, though safely," he added.
"For Claudel poetry was dangerous, for he was in
the world writing of holy things and he came to
think too much of himself."

I had been reading earlier in *Ste. Lydwine*:
"Comprenez-le, vous souffrez parce que vous ne

voulez pas souffrir; le secret de votre détresse est là" (82). Surprisingly he quoted this passage then.

Many Muslims, like many Christians, and others, he said, are too high for Christ's humanity.

"L'exemple de la substitution mystique," he said, quoting *Ste. Lydwine* (80-81), "de la suppléance de celui qui ne doit rien à celui qui doit tout. . . . "

"We save one another through our hearts," he said.

February 14 – Gabrier phoned and insisted I take him to see the painting of Dino Cavallari, about whom I had spoken sometime ago. He said he would drive, though he detested driving through "those areas" of Paris. I considered the opportunity beneficial to Dino. Mistake: to presume to know what might benefit another.

Pierre was in a foul mood. I wondered as he ranted and raved against the communists and prostitutes who inhabited Pigalle and the adjacent *quartiers* through which we sped, if the impoverished radical Léon Bloy had been, as many had testified in that earlier time, as hostile to his caring friends as the bourgeois reactionary Gabrier was now to his.

He turned his gaze from the desolate streets through which he drove as quickly as he could to faraway rich, immoral or amoral America, which he identified inevitably and obviously with me. He cited a "case" pending in California as "very symbolic": that of Caryl Chessman, about whom I knew little or nothing. My ignorance of my country shocked him. He said Chessman is the latest Kafkaesque beetle. Chessman is a victim, like Joseph K. and other Kafka

144

figures, of good intentions, official indecisions, and the inability or refusal of society to bear his crime (he was convicted, I believe, of abduction, rape, and murder of a young woman, though I guessed this only from bits of information barely alluded to during our ride). American society, in this case, wishes to have Chessman take on the guilt of his capital punishment, which Pierre believed was the correct punishment but which he said the society out of sentimentality doesn't wish to believe in. So, it has kept him cruelly and inhumanly on Death Row for thirteen years, setting dates and postponing them, until now the case has entered national politics and, ironically, raises the ghost, Pierre said, of another victim of the same moral refusal, Eddie Slovik, whom Eisenhower waited for "channels" to assume the guilt before he could execute him for the crime of desertion in time in war. Then, he persisted, there's the case of the man who dropped the atomic bomb on Nagasaki, who is going around committing petty and larger crimes to be arrested, found guilty, and punished by a society which finds he did nothing wrong in dropping the bomb but which he finds wrong. Each of these cases, he concluded, points up a certain human sickness, a moral cancer, clinging to America, evasively sentimentalizing certain wilderness and space and other simplistic myths while heading a global machinery of political propaganda based on moral vacuity. He stared at me. I stared back. We drove alongside the giant cemetery of Père Lachaise up the hill toward Place Gambetta and Dino's tiny flat.

Inside, Pierre was exceedingly reserved and formal,

posing a little as an art critic (grotesquely philistine, Dino perceived immediately by the screwed up look on the newcomer's face which suggested both imprecise admiration for the paintings and disgust with the smallness of the flat). He selected two small paintings he *had to have*, rather sentimental ones I thought, one a "Descent from the Cross," the other a somewhat more natural "Flight into Egypt" with a strong undemarcated flow between Virgin and the donkey on which she sat. "Admirably primitive," he said patronizingly; "a genuine interior green," he added authoritatively. He gave the money for both, snatched the paintings to his chest, and said loudly to me "let's go now." Dino offered some aperitif. Pierre refused, saying he had "an appointment." I looked silently at Dino. Francesco was seated quietly at his piano, not playing but rather assessing the stranger with stark, cautious, distant eyes. Pierre hadn't even said hello upon entering, nor did he recognize Francesco's presence and only cursorily Dino's. I felt Dino's look of being invaded, imprisoned, and I realized I could serve our friendship best by getting Pierre out as quickly as possible.

On the way back Pierre told me of a new novella he was writing. It was set in a cemetery. The hero was a prisoner of war returning from Germany to find a twenty-storey building erected on the site where his home had been. No one knew the whereabouts of his wife. He had received notice from her during the war that their daughter had died, and he had nearly despaired. He decides now upon his return to kill himself. Yet he re-reads this letter and learns that the anniversary of his daughter's death is

146

coming due, and so he goes to her grave, one amidst thousands, in the faint hope that his wife will also come. He sees around him on the graves little bouquets of plastic flowers and he realizes his despair. An old woman, wife of the guardian, walks through the rows and finds him down against the graves crying. She talks to him, to a despairing man, of resurrection, but in a very oblique way. The books ends with him seeing flowers growing in the earth, from a grave.

As we crossed the Seine I asked him to let me out there rather than to drop me at home. I wanted to walk alone along the quays for awhile. He said, "But the rain, you'll get wet." I said it was not a cold rain, and I wished him good luck with his novella.

In the evening David Ottoway came over to my flat and we talked a great deal, mostly about America as an "anonymous power," more his subject than mine. Listening to him I feel old though not wise. My mind was still partly divided between Gabrier's obsession with purifying himself of guilt as an imperfect Christian and Massignon's offering of hospitality, two things happening and shared with me in faraway but very real Paris of 1959–1960 and having little or no relevance to America and its ballooning "global consciousness." But David has humility to a degree I lack and I wondered at times why we hadn't changed places, he the guest, I the journalist. Perhaps we had at times, or shared more in common as foreign travelers, witnesses, and friends than either of us then could know. He says he can't imagine bothering important people like Massignon, for he says he has nothing to say. I said

147

I guessed I didn't think about that beforehand, yet I too have nothing to say. I just listen, I said, We agreed maybe that was what it took to enter as guests anywhere.

David's visit was a happy one for me, though I was not used to my own voice and became tired of it quickly. Since we both prefer to listen, we probably won't see that much of each other as things unfold.

He spoke of deGaulle, who interests him very much, he says, as a study in the democratic process at work around a leader: the left moves him in the direction that is moral, he having first the elements of conscience and the courage to be moved or the pressure would only result in violence. Coercion is needed to utilize such a leader's strength, and he must allow the process to proceed, in order to make it work. This fascinates David.

He said of wisdom that it was strange society could not find a similar process of coercion and potentially conscientious leadership to make it more creative in its thinking. For instance, a people ostensibly fond of medicines and idealizing the long life span, instead passively accept retiring their learned men at their first sign of self-awareness, at their first sign of eyelines, at their first fear of becoming "old." He concluded, "that is horrible."

We took a walk together late, rain regardless, and had two hot chocolates in a café.

February 16 — Visit with Père Jean de Menasce, convalescent in his *pavillion* in Neuilly, cared for by Dominican nuns. A remarkable man whom Massignon calls very deep, and loves very much. They are

148

Semitists together, both also now priests through that Semitism, through roots, consonants, texts, tradition, ritual, reverence, worship, prodigious learning. They share a "sense of shame" at uttering vowels, for instance, in the name of G-D, and the experience of being child prodigies with regard to their early grasp of and facility with languages. They also share an attraction to anecdotal histories and a tendency to gossip. Now, following his stroke, Père de Menasce's right side is paralyzed, he drags his right leg as he walks, his right arm hangs down limply, the right side of his face sags, he has lost weight, he speaks with a slur haltingly, but his eyes are keen. He told me Pierre Gabrier comes to see him regularly and he speaks of Massignon and me. He is a man, de Menasce confided without betraying any trust, who suffers greatly from his jealousies and hates himself for what he believes is his moral mediocrity. Read his heart, de Menasce said, not his rhetoric. He is a man in constant pain.

He reminisced a little about his friendship with Maritain and Oppenheimer in Princeton, saying of the latter he was very chagrined ("remorseful," he believed) much of the time, for which he, de Menasce, felt deep compassion with him.

We embraced when we parted in the presence of an old and partially lame but very officious nun who brought him a tray of food and scolded him for letting the last food she brought get cold.

Later, in the evening, Louis telephone me and his "flood of words" included some passing remarks about certain French novelists who try to make romantic heroes out of saints, of Goethe talking of

149

suicide in *Werther*, all of which is divorced from the acts they themselves could commit. He is tired, he said, of romanticism.

He said the actual papers on the dialogues of the Carmelities are far more striking than anything in Bernanos' work: sanctity is not a stage play; not a "performance" or an "acting out of mere ideas." It is devoid of any self-glorification. For a person, he said, to truly illuminate sanctity, he must put his life at every moment in jeopardy and on a fatal call.

These words left me with anxiety, not peace, for I thought I already knew that poetry cannot be molded (at least not by me) only in the service of faith, anymore than faith can be fictionalized, without violence to both.

He spoke more calmly of his daughter, who has collected stories from aged Bretons and Provençals and Acadians in Maine (USA), about which she recently gave a lecture with films before four hundred people. He was unabashedly proud.

February 20—I had lost touch with Arnold Smit, from whom a note just arrived saying that he is entering the Beda College in Rome to become a priest. Cardinal Marella is helping him. He says he is impatient to begin. He is presently living as an oblate (new name: Brother Sebastian) in the Abbaye N.D. du Bec Hellouin (Eure).

February 21—There was a lynching in Paris yesterday. An Algerian killed two policemen and a mob chased and strung up a rope on a lamp post and hung him. He was cut down by policemen but died shortly after.

Cardinal Feltin refused to meet Khrushchev in Notre Dame, choosing to leave the city during the Russian's visit and to leave the hostly duty to deGaulle.

March 3—Note from L.M. dated 2/29/60 (excerpt):

"I agree with you on Cardinals' 'shyness.' You will enjoy at the end of your life the awful 'loneliness' of those who 'weep because they understand.'

"My only living hours are the two hours of Sacrifice, every morning, with its Cross."

He telephoned me late. He told me of some upcoming manifestations for justice in Algeria. But I think he really wanted to tell me something about myself in our ongoing journey together. He said that I was not "a literary man," that he was interested from the beginning in "the spiritual man" in me. Since he often uses the word *literary* in a pejorative way, I took this as a compliment that I don't yet and perhaps never will understand.

He said, as if in a non-sequitur, one must show children their first communion as "a slight breeze," not "a glorious wind."

Then he reverted to the *literary* theme by mentioning an Englishman more or less my age from Oxford who had come to him recently concerning some Huysmans' materials and whom he wanted me to meet. He said the young man at the thought of meeting an American had asked if I was a member of Moral Rearmament, which he dubbed "the crowning sorrow of American thought." He told me the man spoke to him entirely in French, which shows him he came to Christianity through French literature, not prayer. Louis finds this folly, but he liked him nevertheless. He said at the end he doubted he'd keep any rendez-vous with me, for he spoke of "a tennis date *that* day" and he, Louis, hadn't yet proposed a day.

March 17—Mme Abeille phoned. She said she would miss me if I left France. She liked thinking of me as being a friend in Paris even if she didn't see me often. She said her goal of buying M. Marcel's apartment discreetly for him is proceeding slowly. She doesn't know he knows she's doing this. Her call was her way of not asking me for a contribution. She said "sometimes it is harder for some men not to be a priest. Everyone knows what that priest is and either kills him or helps him by hidden sacrifices. For some there is only invisibility."

April 8—Letter from L.M. dated 4/6/60 (excerpt):
"Tom Merton has written me a letter which shows that *Akhbàr al-Hallāj* has shaken him. I would like to have sent him first the *Dīwân*, which is more serene in its *tonalité majeure* and which better shows the Hallajian position and my own. But Tom is not mistaken in believing that my thought can be found through the curve of my life substituted by the Hallajian thought. That is why in order to avoid receiving too profound an impact from it, I have ceased for some years writing on this exceptional personality whose unexpected encounter, fifty years ago, bent my entire life.

Wednesday before Easter—Visit with Louis in his study. He said on April 30 there is to be a demonstration outside the prison at Vincennes where political prisoners are kept illegally and tortured by the government. He has spoken directly with deGaulle, who says he issues orders to stop it and the orders are countermanded by disloyal subordinates. Louis wants to believe him but retains his right of skepticism. The demonstrators (Marcel will join him this time despite his phlebitis) will kneel and pray outside (no one is allowed inside to visit; Louis has a friend in there). I said without hesitation I would join them. He shook his head violently; he said my passport would be taken and I would be deported. He said. "Join us spiritually only. We do not want to send you home nor give any appearance of 'America being involved.' " I understood, but intended to be there in body as well with or without his approval.

April 28—Letter from L.M: dated 4/26/60 in response to a note of my own in which I confided my decision to leave France in June (excerpt):

Dear Friend,

I understand your anguish before this return to the USA, and I could share it, if I hadn't found for you that you have to end your Gilgamesh (did you see what Bowra says of him?), and that is an internal remedy: anywhere.

In the afternoon (of the 30th) I shall be at the meeting, and afterwards . . . well, I don't think my

153

freedom shall be caught. Alas, G. Marcel writes that on Saturday he shall be in the south for the "Réarmament Moral," but that "spiritually" he shall be at Vincennes.

We have been singled for loneliness by Our Lord, for "soledad": even after death?

Fraternally,
Louis M.

April 29—I am not sure why these discontinuous thoughts: I have to make "anywhere" a place where I am afraid to go. This old companion fear returns. A poet can respond to birds but cannot fly. The cycle of Gilgamesh includes the watering place among the animals, the opening of the traps, the final bathing at the serpent's pool, where there are tears at the vision of mortality, not tears at the vision of immortality.

Why does Utnapishtim look downcast? Why is immortality so mournful?

"We must raise the dead out of their graves. . . . "

I remember Louis's appearance at the Sorbonne that first time I saw him, at the forum for peace in Algeria. He was the dynamic one, the one who spoke last, who shied away from having his photograph taken afterwards: deep creases in his face, white hair, a stern, heroic profile; and when he laughed during his speech, which was the most alive, longest, and least pretentious or *literary* of all the speeches, it was the laughter of someone who had cried at both visions.

Now that evening comes back to me. I'm afraid I am collecting memories. Now I know I am leaving.

April 30—Gabrier came to see me as I was leaving my flat to join the demonstration at Vincennes. I didn't understand why he was there and became anxiously aware of time.

"Can we talk?" he asked.

In my confusion I said "no" first, then "yes."

We sat facing each other in the living room, he on the couch, I on a chair. For a long time we didn't speak. I struggled not to look at my watch.

Gradually the meaning of the unexpected visit, like so many things I experienced in France, became clear.

If like Gabrier himself I had been engaged in a series of fictionalizations of my states of anxiety, I might have imagined him saying something horrifying about why the French are justified in torturing Algerians—thus making my anxiety intensify even further, irony run rampant, the rest. But he said nothing. His silence was more terrible. I knew I couldn't leave him alone.

May 1—Louis phoned this morning. He asked me if I knew of a translator (even I myself) who might translate "an important book" on Maritain. I wanted only news of yesterday. He said, as if incidentally, that the "meeting" was a success and an "anniversary" for him (of his imprisonment in Iraq). But he gave few details. He said he "knew" I was there in spirit. He said when they were in prison (in prison?) a woman brought them lilies of the valley. Outside when they were on the sidewalk, policemen took their names. Among them was a Danish journalist who was deported.

May 2—Caryl Chessman was executed today.

155

May 10—A visit to a church: St. Antoine des Quinze-vingts, 57 rue Traversière, Paris 12.

In a workers' area, near Gare de Lyon, and an overpass, opposite a garage. The interior choir of the church was locked, but behind the closed grate I could see the altar, not an unusual one perhaps but to my present state strangely beautiful. There was a young woman sitting to my left on one of the benches. I steadied my eyes on the altar and the arches over the side chapels and said the prayer that had welled up in me over the past three years in France—prayers for friends and, today, of personal surrender.

The sound of trains passing nearby overhead was deafening.

May 11—Received a note from Jean de Menasce dated May 9 from Kantonsspital, Lucerne. He will come back to Neuilly in autumn. "Remember me in your prayers as I do you in mine." He also mentioned the Maritain book (by Bars: *M. in his Time*) and offered to look for a USA publisher.

I was shocked by this letter—*l'esprit bouleversé*. . . . I thought I was losing my mind. I could not have visited Jean in his *pavillon* in February for he hadn't returned to Paris and wouldn't until autumn. Somehow I had combined my concern for his health, my imagining of what his condition must be after his stroke, and my recollection of a visit to the *pavillon* once when the old nun came in with a tray, to form another visit that didn't take place. I remember him saying those things about Gabrier, Maritain, and Oppenheimer. But mostly, at this moment, I realize my gross credulity and it frightens me.

May 12—The annual Huysmans Society mass at St. Séverin, 8:45 a.m. Daniel-Rops pronounced the *discours d'usage* in the garden afterwards: near the medallion of Huysmans made by Massignon's father, Pierre Roche (pseudonym). Other of his works—sculptures—are found in the Luxembourg gardens and other parks in Paris. It is an old family that has given much of itself to France since before the Revolution. Many gathered at the mass, some I knew, including Louis, some I didn't. They are mostly old, several enfeebled, a few younger; French and foreign; some agnostics, some esthetes, some believers. Everyone seems to have his or her private link to some stage in Huysmans' itinerary, which was long and complex and carefully documented: from naturalism and discipleship to Zola, to self-exploration, absorption with the senses, decadence, Satanism and the black mass, despair, conversion, convalescence, the vocation of oblate, historian and critic of Gregorian chant, monastic discipline, church art and architecture, of pilgrim to Lourdes, of hagiographer and witness of mystical substitution, unto his own final suffering—an itinerary which he himself said was a lifelong quest for spiritual honesty and sincerity, shared at different points by those present but which his critics believe he never achieved. One book of his I especially admired was his early *Croquis Parisiens*, sketches of corners of Paris made with a painter's eye for color, mood, detail, the book that the Englishman with the tennis date is translating.

June 7—A long letter from Merton dated June 1 (excerpt):

I have written to Maritain to put in a word for you as translator. But still if you do not want to do the job I see no reason why you should have to. . . . Your own creative work is more important and should come first, unless you need money badly or something like that.

Louis asked me to pray on some special day, for he intends to begin something to do with Africa. . . . I picked June 3 as a day to say a mass for him. . . . My heart is very much in Africa.

Poor Pasternak has died. His story has ended and remains to be understood. . . .

Let us think more about the role of America in all this. I have been feeling rather negative and discouraged, but I realize how little I see and understand. All I know is that I have an overwhelming feeling that we are missing the boat because we have been blinded by money and love of material things. Yet there is always the blank, innocent, patient, absurd good will. How good is it, that is the question? I wonder if the answer is not just that we have always rather humbly imagined that we were good because we suspected we might be fools. But now that we are convinced we are perhaps not fools but very smart people are we going to commit the sin of deducing goodness from our supposed wisdom? If so. . . .

June 9—Last visit with Gabrier. We had dinner out. We ate and talked uncomfortably. We could not reconcile. He has built a personal "politique" out of loss into an isolation in which he is terrified of the next event whatever it is: he is haunted by the martyrdom of France. He recited the Occupation, Indochina, Algeria, crime in the streets, a photograph of

Brigitte Bardot's bust on the Champs-Elysées . . . and then accused me, the representative of "America," of isolationism. If "I" were to come in on France's side now, instead of supporting Massignon's position, France would keep Algeria and Europe would be more secure with its own oil pipeline. He was upset over recent "pacifist" statements made by Senator Kennedy on Algeria. "Massignon," he said, "is a traitor to France. He cites Muslims, Gandhi, known decadents like Huysmans as friends and authorities. Huysmans was not a saint," he said. "Massignon's a fool!" It was a dinner that became increasingly indigestible with each bite.

When we left the restaurant we walked out along the Quai de Montebello and stood for a few minutes in silence looking at the Seine and across at Notre-Dame. His eyes glistened and he had the frightened look he had in my flat on the day of the Vincennes demonstration. When he turned he said in his worst broken English (which he rarely used), "I hope we are friends."

I said, "Yes, I too."

June 10—Brief note from Louis dated June 8:

My dear friend,

the date of your departure is near and we did not meet as planned June 3. Telephone me so we may meet again before you leave.

Affectionately,
Louis

No sleep for three nights. Now I shall fail the test of Utnapishtim: I shall be unable to keep awake for eternal life.

June 11—Yvonne came in from Brittany to see me. She came from seeing Louis at his place. She said he enters others' universes ("the true fullness of love") without ever forgetting a detail of each. Whereas poor Gabrier refuses others' universes. She said sadly that publishers are refusing to consider Gabrier's work because of his political fanaticism, which has ruined its quality. He is near Oedipus' despair, accusing others of his blindness. She said she can't visit him now without having a priest along. People are withdrawing from him . . . as people are beginning to admit the tortures of Algerians, which he denied officially as Inspector of Prisons. She said bitterly, "They admit the tortures but they still insist they are necessary. Pierre's position is still popular, though he is not. They have left him, the Inspector who denied the truth and now he is terrified of the truth everybody knows."

I believe she told me this to bring cloture to an old friendship of her own with Gabrier that she feared might be our only link. Or she wanted me, as I leave, to know where she stands definitively between Gabrier and Massignon. She told me of two abbeys that were racist centers in her country, and told me many other things so rapidly that I can't remember. It was all too much to absorb and, in any case, she said "The salvation of the world does not depend on 'La France.' "

She asked me to pray for her son who has three months left in Algerian service, then he is to marry. She said he is ready spiritually for whatever might happen to him in Algeria, but she is afraid for his body.

She said she believed, though it was a hard belief to always support, in forgiveness. "Never under any circumstances can revenge be justified. Never," she repeated, "or one fails to remain in the moment of one's calling."

We embraced in silence and I began in her arms to feel the first real pain of leaving.

Later I went to Mme Abeille's grand apartment to say good-bye. She was sitting with a cat in her lap in the antique-filled, sunless living room. She spoke of the voices she could still hear in the room, the diminishing numbers of "grands orateurs" these days, and her desire at times to clear away the past. . . . She fears her dear "maître Gabriel Marcel" will be kicked out of his apartment if he can't buy it—and he has no money, but he will be hurt and humiliated if she buys it alone for him—and so few have contributed. She cried a little, barely audibly.

I thought to myself: I will be useless to my friends if I remain to admire them. But is it possible to think of never seeing them again?

After a shy but warm parting, I left her place and walked through the Jardin du Luxembourg past the bust of Charles Baudelaire:

> Oh c'est vraiment, Seigneur
> Le meilleur témoignage
> Que nous puissons donner
> de croire digne

Que cet ardent sanglot
　　Qui roule d'âge en âge
　Et vient mourir au bord
　　de votre éternité. . . .

June 16 — Last visit with Louis Massignon
It was after a day spent at the station, paying bills,
leaving off books, tiring and sad. I am pretending it
does not hurt to leave one's friends. I could not see
Dino, Julienne, and Francesco, for they are on a visit
to Dino's ailing mother in Italy. I spoke on the phone
with Daniélou, who said he would be coming to
America soon. Whether true or not, it made the
ocean seem smaller than I know it is.

Louis sat in his chair behind his desk, as always,
and I sat on the couch by the window. Papers were
strewn over the desk and he had been typing one of
his "Bulletins" when I arrived. He handed me a book
that had just been delivered to his door — *Fishbelly* by
the American writer-in-exile Richard Wright with the
author's handwritten inscription inside "To Louis
Massignon, a friend."

Louis seemed to study me very carefully, then said
"Your Gilgamesh is the way for you. It is the most
profound expression of the human soul, for it is of
immortality. But condense it," he warned, "don't
make it *a great epic*, which is past, but tell it as a
simple truth, which does not age in time." I realized
he had helped me find the great secret in it, which
could not be written or divulged in so many words:
the sudden instant of Gilgamesh's losing of the plant
is the simultaneous gift of immortality to the dead
friend he prayed for. It is the new (unwritten) voyage into suffering and selflessness.

162

"For some reason," he said, "it has fallen to you to make these voyages: out of your country to another, into suffering, to immortality. And this is the union of friendship that reaches also," he particularized, "through many Semitic and Oriental souls."

He said many things, prophetic things about the world, and spoke of God being beside and away, high and low, not only small but also large, unconfinable yet intimate. . . . He said for him memory supports continuing moments of divine relation. Yet he does not wish for joy that he knows will end. He read me a passage from a 1940 notebook he kept on a visit to Yugoslavia. He spoke of the dangers he saw then. He recalled a visit to La Salette where he sought for himself a deeper gift of compassion for others. "Even from Heaven she gives tears."

He spoke of poor Gabrier as a Shakespearean tragic figure, a man so intelligent yet caught in the occasional lies of hierarchy, where lies are more horrible.

He read me a mocking press clipping about a recent demonstration: "Even a Collège de France professor got down in the sidewalk dirt with those non-violents." He smiled as if he'd received an honorary degree. He said he recently went to court at the request of the wife of a Jewish communist who had the courage to write about those who tortured him. He, Louis, was there with the head of the Communist Party, a radical socialist, and a member of deGaulle's intimates—four witnesses on the man's behalf. DeGaulle, he says, has told him of their closeness now in thought. Yesterday he spoke again in public for Algerian independence.

He stopped talking and sat back in his chair looking at me. He seemed to be very tired suddenly, yet his eyes were wide and alert and attentive. Perhaps he was tired of France, the world, or just talking about it all and knew it was not what had drawn us together before or now.

It was late in the afternoon, but not one of our long visits. I sensed he would like to have it last longer, as would I have, but he stood up and I stood up. We laughed awkwardly together and then he embraced me and kissed me on either cheek. I felt pain in my heart then and was struggling for composure.

We walked together through the hallway to the front door of his apartment. Outside by the elevator, after I pushed the call button, he leaned back with his hands behind him holding the stair railing. When the elevator came I turned to face him but he continued to look down. Our eyes met only when I was inside and the doors were closing.

Afterwards I found myself in the old *Quartier Latin* again but I did not know how, nor how such affection of my friends could make me forget where I was going. Oldness of surroundings no longer made me dream. I had the passage home on a ship and, by adoption of a familiar myth, I knew seductive voices would be heard on the sea and already I had to be tied to a mast to resist their sounds.

When I returned to my flat I sat down with one of the offprints Louis had given me months before entitled "*Voyelles Sémitiques et Sémantique Musicale.*" It was formal and forbidding. But it carried his voice.

It included reproductions of two paintings by Arab

painters, each in the form of musical notations but in fact they were calligraphies of Arabic texts, representing abstract silhouettes of the sacred name of God — in black for the unpronounced Arabic consonants, as if skeletal; in red for the vocalizing and vivifying vowels, representing the spirit of the words. Together they formed a rhythmic contour of successive varied waves across the light sand-colored page, moving from right to left, creating a melodic atmosphere.

Louis wrote in this article of the darkness one encounters in approaching the past. The only light one has is given by words intoned from it. The intonation reveals their intentions. There is a music that both precedes and follows the words emerging from silence.

It is not in our own culture cherished in isolation that we can realize this phenomenon, he wrote, but only in crossing over to another that forces us to listen, to understand through hearing and, only then, translating. When we hear no longer only our own masters but the sounds of a distant city, the rhythmic refrains issuing from the depths of the unrefined and unrecorded masses, revealing their sounds, their cries, their proverbs, we are at the source of language, the origin of the idea, the creative intent, which colors and gives life to form.

I set down the offprint and thought back to my own childhood when I sought, as if from a distant country, the lost sound of my deceased father's voice. At age seven I sought but I could not cross over to it. The only light providing life and harmony to form crossed over naturally instead to me: in the

165

sun's slow descent along the river near our Maryland home and across it through the flat reed beds on the other side, lingering in a reddish orange afterglow spread wide at the edge of the horizon where two rivers met leaving a residue of violet and rose at the center of my vision, where it seemed to remain a moment longer as if to form an unspoken word in the incoming darkness.

Sacred texts, I resumed reading, are music written; lives of saints are music sung. It is on the threshold of death, of absolute silence, of total poverty of self, that language and music are reunited in the simplest, briefest of words, of outcries. . . .

For a few moments I lapsed into my memories. I remembered many of the occasions when we were together. Now I wanted him to talk again without any pre-planned subject or reason for talking apart from sharing his learning and his presence with a friend.

I imagined we were together. He was in his chair in the windowlight that flowed to the center of the narrow high-ceilinged room. I stared at him shyly, as always, for I did not feel I could presume on his friendship. Would he speak about the Algerian laborer whose hands had been crushed? The silence of my flat was overwhelming to me as I looked for presences in vain. I even asked a question, as if to begin the conversation. It was about al-Hallaj, the subject and "friend" of his lifework from whom he had often drawn his thoughts and point of view. "Did he *desire* martyrdom?" I wanted to hear him explain.

"He was willing to die for love," I heard his voice or the voice of his writings accompanying me in

166

solitude, "and in that sense he desired death for himself or for that part of the self that created distance between himself and his Beloved. He wished to end the idol of himself, the self he was looking at in his solitude instead of looking at his loved One. He was tired of false love, of loving falsehood, of seeming lovable to anyone. He longed to be beyond the world of himself. But his love was also of justice, of truth, and for this his death was made as an offering for others who hungered after both. It was a substitution for them, uniting enemies together against him whom they did not understand and despised. He even risked damnation for such love: damned in this world surely, and willing to be damned in the next if it would end division and injustice between men by serving as an object for their common wrath. That is substitution: the taking on of suffering for others' liberation from themselves. Only a few are lovers at such extremes of love."

AFTERWORD

As was mentioned in the Foreword to Part Two, I have included here only a selection of entries from the diary. My association with Louis Massignon and his work did not end with my leaving Paris in 1960. And though I never saw him again, our friendship continued through letters and interest in each other sustained through less overt means, and indeed survived his death on October 31, 1962. At the time of his death, I was beginning in America a graduate program of studies in the civilization of the Islam that had nurtured al-Hallaj, with the purpose of one day translating my friend's lifework. Later in the same year, I met Jack Barrett, from whom I learned of Bollingen Foundation's long-standing commitment to publish a translation of the awaited second edition of *La Passion* in English. Our mutual goals merged in 1968 when Barrett contracted me to undertake the project and came to fruition with the publication of the four volumes in 1983, regrettably after Barrett's own death. In the early years of labor on these volumes I also completed my retelling of the Gilgamesh story, which was published in 1970 with one of Dino Cavallari's paintings on the cover.

Completion of these works was possible only through the impetus of friendship as recalled in the present volume.

The correspondence between the two figures of

Gilgamesh and al-Hallaj, the one mythical, the other historical, comes from the figure of the older sage whom in the one the journeyer seeks, who in the other the journeyer is. In the end, however, such narrative testimonies perhaps have only the simplicity of this theme in common. It was not my intent to make distinct civilizations appear comparable or blurred into vapid "universal" similarity, but to respond to certain human values reverberating from specific sources, perhaps only coincidentally, in each. It may also have been merely chance that Massignon and I met. What matters in any case to me is that we did meet and that our meeting has borne fruit that we believed from the beginning would be of value to others.

My intent in the present "memoir" was to recount the beginning of the friendship that bore this fruit, and thereby to evoke and extend to others simply and directly the person and presence of Louis Massignon.